• Dog Breed Handbooks •

GOLDEN
RETRIEVER

• DOG BREED HANDBOOKS •

GOLDEN RETRIEVER

DR. BRUCE FOGLE

SPECIAL PHOTOGRAPHY BY
TRACY MORGAN

DORLING KINDERSLEY
LONDON · NEW YORK · STUTTGART · MOSCOW

A DORLING KINDERSLEY BOOK

Project Editor PHIL HUNT
Art Editor WENDY BARTLET
Editor SARAH LILLICRAPP
Designer HELEN THOMPSON
Managing Editor FRANCIS RITTER
Managing Art Editor DEREK COOMBES
DTP Designer CRESSIDA JOYCE
Production Controller RUTH CHARLTON

First published in Great Britain in 1996
by Dorling Kindersley Limited,
9 Henrietta Street, London WC2E 8PS

Visit us on the World Wide Web at
http://www.dk.com

A CIP catalogue record for this book is
available from the British Library

ISBN 0 7513 0340 2

Reproduced by Colourscan, Singapore
Printed and bound in Italy by Graphicom

CONTENTS

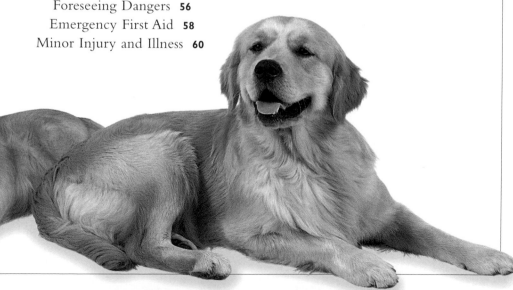

INTRODUCTION

WE LIKE TO THINK that humans domesticated the dog, but this is only partly true. The dog has been our partner for longer than any other species of animal. It has guarded our homes, assisted in the hunt, pulled our heavy loads, even been a source of clothing and food in famine, but we did not actively domesticate it. Around 12,000 years ago, our ancestors in Asia created sites of permanent habitation.

It seems difficult to believe that the wolf is a relative, albeit distant, of the lovable Golden Retriever

Local Asiatic wolves – sociable by nature – were attracted to these settlements and moved into the surrounding areas to scavenge for food. Only the smallest and tamest wolves were successful in adapting to the new ecological environment, domesticating themselves in order to survive.

ADAPTATION OF THE BREEDS

By about 6,000 years ago, selective breeding by humans had produced many different dog breeds, from companionable miniatures to giant dogs of war. More recently, in the

19th-century aristocrats developed the Golden Retriever from early sporting dogs such as these

last 1,000 years humankind has created the time, wealth, and weaponry to hunt purely for pleasure, and this has led to the development of the sporting dog. The Golden Retriever is an excellent example of this most advanced branch of canines, because it performs in an unnatural way – adeptly finding wounded and freshly-killed prey, but rather than instinctively eating it, carefully bringing the game back to its waiting master.

The modern Golden Retriever relishes the chance to retrieve from water, a reflection of its Water Spaniel origins

One of the most docile of all the dog breeds, the Golden Retriever prefers lounging to guarding

THE IDEAL COMPANION

The Golden Retriever is a lively dog that enjoys the exhilaration of outdoor activity as much as it does the relaxation of being at home. By nature, the Golden is generally placid and friendly, seeking the company of other dogs or people for frivolous play. It is this affectionate, even temperament which draws most people to the breed, but if you require guarding services rather than companionship, choose another breed.

GOLDEN RETRIEVERS TODAY

The modern Golden Retriever was developed during the last century to meet growing demands for a superb sporting breed – to work to the gun and retrieve game for huntsmen. Its specific abilities have, however, led to a variety of other roles. Goldens can be found helping the disabled and infirm in their daily lives, all over the world. As guide dogs, pure-bred Goldens and their Labrador cross-breeds act as eyes for the blind, guiding their owners safely

Selective breeding has honed the Golden's natural skills, making it an invaluable assistance dog

through busy streets. The Golden is just as successful in the role of hospital visitor, where its naturally affable character promotes therapeutic results in many patients. But for most devotees of the breed, the Golden Retriever's most attractive attribute is its generous nature – it never tires of company and is always eager to please all family members.

Whatever the role – whether gundog, assistance dog, or family pet – the Golden Retriever is one of the most celebrated and popular breeds

THE IDEAL CHOICE

THE GENTLE, RESPONSIVE GOLDEN RETRIEVER has a well-deserved reputation as a family companion, but commitment from the owner is essential. Make sure you are willing to cope with the Golden's lively, sometimes excitable nature, its great need for exercise, and its continuously shedding hair.

PART OF THE FAMILY

Remember that your cute, fluffy puppy will grow into a large, vigorous dog, who will need looking after for up to 15 years. Like a child, it depends on you to provide its nutrition, education, and overall well-being. Consider the amount of time you can dedicate to your dog, the space available in your home, the cost of veterinary attention, and most importantly, your dog's essential food requirements – Goldens are among the dog world's greatest eaters!

A HAPPY AND BOISTEROUS BREED

A BOUNDING "HELLO"
If Goldens are not trained early in life to keep all four feet on the ground, you and your friends can expect a very warm welcome from this friendly but sometimes clumsy breed. Choose a Golden only if you can accept such affection and the odd broken object caused by its wagging tail.

IRREPRESSIBLE RETRIEVERS
Goldens are natural retrievers who cannot resist picking up stray items, especially those with an interesting odour. Consider a Golden only if you are prepared to be extra tidy, or if you are amenable to having shoes, socks, and even undergarments presented to both family members and visiting friends.

NATURAL LOVE OF WATER

Although now a popular pet, Goldens were originally bred to work outdoors, retrieving in rivers and thick undergrowth. Therefore, no stream or dirty puddle can be passed without investigation, requiring you to clean your dog and your car on a regular basis.

PREPARE FOR HAIR!

If you prefer to dress in dark colours, the Golden Retriever can be an exasperating companion. No matter how fastidious you are, its soft, blond hair has a tendency to stick to most fabrics, making it difficult to remove from clothing, upholstery, and carpets. A Golden, therefore, is perhaps not the best dog for the exceptionally house-proud. Dogs that live outdoors in kennels moult twice a year, but those kept in centrally-heated environments tend to shed their hair all year round. However, these problems can be overcome with a slight alteration to your home life, combined with a daily grooming routine to keep the loose hair under control.

A REWARDING COMPANION

If you want a good-natured, sociable dog, then a Golden Retriever is ideal. Selective breeding has created this potential, but it is only through appropriate training that these desirable traits can be developed. Without good training, some Goldens may show possessive tendencies towards toys or food. Start teaching your Golden from an early age that all toys and food belong to you, and possessiveness should not arise.

Owner chats while well-trained Golden interacts with other dog

BREED CHARACTERISTICS

THE GOLDEN RETRIEVER'S FIRST breed standard was written by people who recognized its potential as an excellent gundog. Even today, the breed standard continues to emphasize the Golden's body conformation, which is eminently suited for pace and endurance in the field. Its friendly, eager-to-please nature is equally important to this working role.

BALANCED FOR ACTION
The Golden's body is streamlined and naturally proportioned for smooth, free-striding action. Balance is evident in the size of the head and neck relative to the body, making it ideal for carrying game.

SKULL
Broad skull, with defined indentation at base of muzzle. Medium-length, powerful jaws hold teeth in complete "scissors" bite

NECK
Sturdy and muscular, with clean, firm lines

FOREQUARTERS
Long and sloping, supported by strong-boned forelegs; perfectly straight from elbow to ground

ROBUST BODY
Viewed from the side, the Golden's physique is obviously that of a hunter – powerfully built, with fore- and hind legs in excellent proportion to the body. This leaves the Golden superbly equipped for long periods of work over variable terrain, as does its weather-resistant coat.

EARS
Close-hanging, rather short ears, set on level with eyes

EYES
Friendly, medium-sized brown eyes are placed well apart

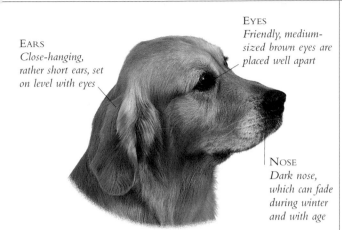

NOSE
Dark nose, which can fade during winter and with age

DIVERGING BREED STANDARDS

The differences in height and coat colour that exist between the Golden Retriever's breed standard in various countries are minimal. The American standard calls for slightly larger dogs with rich, golden coats – never very dark or very pale. The British standard calls for slightly smaller dogs, and allows coats in any shade of gold or cream. Interpretation of the various standards is flexible enough to allow successful dogs from one country to be used in breeding programmes in another. It is the overall temperament and physique that remains central to the Golden's widespread success.

GOOD-NATURED, DEVOTED COMPANION
The Golden Retriever's eager, alert disposition is obvious from both its facial expression and the shape of its body. Its naturally friendly personality is frequently shown with a canine "smile", a characteristic emphasized by the dark pigmentation of the lip folds.

BACK
Top line of body is strong and level

DOUBLE COAT
Flat or wavy outer coat with good feathering covers dense, waterproof down

TAIL
Medium-length tail is very thick at base, gradually tapering to tip, with heavy feathering on underside

HINDQUARTERS
Broad, muscular, and very strongly developed, slightly sloping to tail, with sturdy thighs

FEET
Round, compact, "cat-like" feet are well knuckled on thick pads

MEASUREMENTS (BRITISH BREED STANDARD)
Height at withers (see page 77):
FEMALE 51–56 cm (20–22 in)
MALE 56–61 cm (22–24 in)
Weight, in proportion to height:
FEMALE 25–29.5 kg (55–65 lb)
MALE 29.5–34 kg (65–75 lb)

1.8 m (6 ft)

BEHAVIOUR PROFILE

EVERY DOG'S PERSONALITY is shaped in part by its early experiences within the litter, and later with you. Heredity is equally important, which is why, regardless of upbringing, each breed has its own behaviour profile. Overall, the Golden Retriever makes an ideal family companion.

TRAINABILITY/OBEDIENCE

Golden Retrievers are among the most trainable of all breeds, surpassed only by the Labrador Retriever and German Shepherd. Originally bred to work under human direction, Golden Retrievers respond well to instruction and show loyalty to their owners.

PLAYFULNESS WITH OTHER DOGS

Gundogs were bred to work in harmony with other dogs in the field, and are therefore the most playful canine group. The Golden Retriever comes a very close second to the Labrador Retriever as the most social and interactive breed.

BARKING TO PROTECT THE HOME

Other than the Newfoundland and Labrador (both close relatives of the Golden), there is no breed rated poorer at barking to defend its home than the Golden Retriever. Goldens are more likely to show burglars to the family jewels rather than protect them!

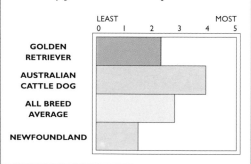

NEED FOR PHYSICAL ACTIVITY

Coming from a working background, the Golden thrives on physical and mental activity. Only the Australian Kelpie, Australian Cattle Dog, and Chesapeake Bay Retriever have a greater need, although early experience influences this trait even more than heredity.

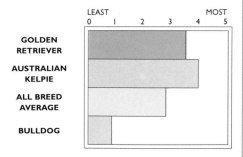

How to Use the Behaviour Charts

In a recent study, vets and dog breeders have assessed over 100 breeds, rating each on a scale of 0–5 for specific personality traits, with 0 representing the lowest score among all dogs and 5 the highest. Here, for eight different behaviours, the Golden Retriever is compared with the statistically "average" canine, as well as with breeds rated at both extremes for each characteristic. The findings below do not take the dog's sex into consideration.

Reliable with Strange Children

The amiable Golden Retriever is grouped with the most dependable of all breeds when meeting unfamiliar children. Even so, an adult should always be present, and children, until emotionally mature, should never be left alone even with the gentlest of dogs.

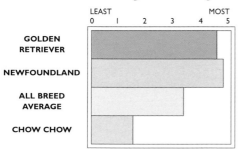

Calm in New Circumstances

Goldens, in common with Newfoundlands, Labrador Retrievers, Cairn Terriers, and French Bulldogs, tend to be unperturbed by strange sounds, surroundings, or people. This trait reflects the breed's development as a gundog with an adaptable, easy-going nature.

Destructive when Alone

Goldens are slightly more likely than the "average" dog to be destructive when left alone. All dogs are less prone to behaviour such as scratching on walls, digging in carpets, or chewing furniture when well exercised and given stimulating toys.

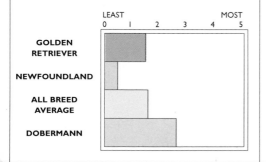

House Trainable

Most dogs respond fairly well to house training, and the Golden is surpassed only by the German Shepherd and Labrador. These three breeds have a great aptitude for learning, a general eagerness to please, and exceptionally willing, dutiful characters.

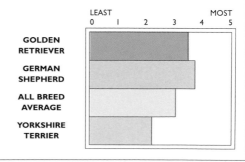

COATS AND COLOURS

MRS. WINIFRED CHARLESWORTH, a founding member of the first Golden Retriever Club, wrote that Goldens should look like, "ripe fields of wheat, oats and barley". Some do, but colours can also range from creamy white to golden red, with smooth or wavy coats. Both colour and texture alter with age.

COLOUR VARIATIONS

Colour has become a controversial topic among Golden Retriever breeders. The British standard allows for any shade of gold or cream, but neither red nor mahogany, while the American breed standard limits the range to various shades of rich and lustrous gold, and disqualifies all very pale or dark individuals. This "light cream" may be frowned upon in the show ring, but it has become extremely popular in the UK and Europe, and is similar in shade to the original Goldens bred in Scotland by Lord Tweedmouth. If your Golden is not destined for the show ring, make a choice purely on personal preference.

RICH, GOLDEN COLOURING
This dog exemplifies the colour preferred by some breeders.

SHADES OF GOLD
Colour intensity ranges from the fashionable champagne cream through to deep, golden–red.

COLOUR PREDICTION
Puppies have light downy hair; the shade of the ear tips should indicate mature coat colour, but check its parents to estimate its adult coat texture.

Changes in Coat Texture

The first coat for many Goldens is flat and glossy, but as the feathers develop, and after several moults, some coats become wavier. Spaying can occasionally alter the female's coat; it sometimes promotes thick, lustrous growth, or it can diminish the coat's natural shine. The male's usually dense coat may become thinner, making it easier to manage.

AGEING MALE
Although his expression is still keen, white facial hair indicates that this male is growing old.

THICK, CURLY COAT
This type of coat is typical in older Goldens, and is a reminder of its water dog origins.

FULL, LUSTROUS COAT
The feathers have grown quickly in this spayed female, and they will require regular trims.

Natural-born Swimmers

DENSE, WATERPROOF UNDERCOAT
Through selective breeding – perhaps from Canadian ancestors that needed to survive in the icy waters of Newfoundland – the Golden Retriever has developed a thick, woolly undercoat. This gives superb, waterproof insulation, although severe conditions can still cause hypothermia.

A BREED THAT REVELS IN GETTING WET
From puddles to lakes and rivers to oceans, water is an irresistible temptation for any Golden. The breed's powerful legs and well-proportioned chest make swimming sheer pleasure. Bathing, however, is another matter; clean water and shampoo are not nearly as exhilarating as revelling in mud and slime.

SEX AND TYPE DIFFERENCES

MALE AND FEMALE Golden Retrievers differ not only in the obvious physical ways, but also in temperament and behaviour. Individual variations can also be seen between the character and trainability of those Goldens bred for companionship, the show ring, and working roles.

PHYSIQUE AND TEMPERAMENT: THE SEXES COMPARED

Male Goldens are typically larger and more powerfully built than females, and have less delicate features. In behaviour, gender-related differences are very minor, with males only slightly more dominant. Overall, both sexes are very even-tempered and highly trainable.

Overall, female body is shorter and slighter than male's

Female head is smaller, with delicate features

GENTLE, RESPONSIVE FEMALE
Female Goldens are considered to be easier to train than males, and are less likely to disobey their owners. They also appear to be more playful with other dogs. Even when spayed, the female Golden Retriever shows little personality change, remaining affable with an intense desire to please.

GENDER-SPECIFIC MEDICAL PROBLEMS

A variety of diseases are caused or influenced by sex hormones. Unless spayed early in life, females of all breeds may suffer from breast cancer and pyometra, or womb infection. Uncastrated males sometimes develop perianal tumours, testicular cancer, or prostate disorders, with associated pain or bleeding on urination. Neutering is part of the preferred treatment for all gender-related medical conditions, but – particularly in Goldens – it must be followed by careful diet control to prevent weight gain.

CONFIDENT MALE
Males tend to be more assertive than their female counterparts, which can sometimes lead to wilful behaviour and disobedience. Some display a possessive and suspicious nature by guarding their food or toys, and by barking to protect the home from strangers – not usually a strong trait in either sex. These characteristics can all be controlled by specific training.

SHOW OR WORKING TYPE?

"PERFECT" LOOKS
Goldens destined for the show ring are specifically bred to meet show standards. At one time, there was a single worldwide breed standard, but recently minor differences have developed between some countries. For example, Goldens in the US are slightly larger, with coat colours restricted within a smaller "golden palette" than that of their European relatives. This has led to a specifically defined American breed standard. Regardless of which standard is used, show dogs are bred primarily for beauty and then trained from an early age in show-ring deportment.

Broad, chiselled head with kindly expression

Strong, well-feathered tail is carried level, sometimes curling upwards at the end

Stocky, muscular build with well-developed chest and powerful hindquarters

Slimmer, lighter frame is suited to nimble activity in the field

BRED TO WORK
While it is possible to train all Golden Retrievers for working trials in obedience, agility, scent trailing, or as gundogs, some are specifically bred for this work. Although their leaner, lighter bodies are considered to be more agile in the field, they may still meet show standards. Working dogs are also bred to possess an enhanced retrieving ability and a keen responsiveness to specialized training.

SELECTIVE BREEDING FOR SPECIAL ROLES

Pure-bred Golden Retrievers, Labrador Retrievers, and Golden/Labrador crosses are the world's most popular and successful assistance dogs. Known primarily as guide dogs for the blind, Goldens are also selectively bred in the US, The Netherlands, and United Kingdom to assist people whose everyday mobility is restricted to a wheelchair.

Golden guide dog is sound worker with naturally helpful character

FINDING THE RIGHT DOG

HAVING DECIDED TO SHARE your home with a Golden Retriever, be selective in your search. Seek professional advice from your local veterinarian or dog training club, and consider your lifestyle; you will then be in the best position to choose. Any purchase should incorporate a thorough health check by your vet.

ADVICE ON WHERE TO BUY AND WHAT TO LOOK FOR

CONSULT A VETERINARIAN
Vets and their staff are an excellent source of free, unbiased information on what to look for and where to find a healthy Golden Retriever. They are often aware of the breed's medical problems and any behavioural idiosyncracies that may arise.

INQUIRE AT LOCAL DOG TRAINING CLUBS
Trainers at a local dog club can supply helpful guidance on how to recognize a trainable Golden. They may also recommend breeders who produce dogs specifically for field work or showing. While gender partly determines a dog's temperament, so do breeding lines.

SUITABLE FOR YOUR LIFESTYLE?

The Golden Retriever is a big, hairy dog, with a notably high demand for mental and physical activity. If you have never owned a large dog, try spending some time with one to get an idea of its feeding, exercise, and space requirements. Unless you live alone, buying a dog is a joint decision. Make sure all the family are involved in the search for the right dog.

Owner and children treat pet Golden as well-loved member of family

DECIDING ON A PUPPY OR AN ADULT DOG

BUYING A PURE-BRED PUPPY

Remember, puppies are undoubtedly appealing, but they require plenty of early attention. Take your time to choose, and visit several reputable breeders with new litters, noting the general physique and temperament of the mother and, if possible, the father as well. Control your impulse to buy the first puppy that catches your eye; it may well be the best, but you can only be sure after seeing others.

ANIMAL RESCUE CENTRES

If you prefer the idea of getting an adult dog, without the inconvenience of puppy training, then an animal shelter is a good source. An abandoned Golden is rare; a rescued one is more likely to have behavioural problems, notably destructive activity when left alone. Yet, these dogs can make loyal, affectionate companions – just be prepared to cope with any personality quirks.

HEALTH CHECKS FOR YOUR NEW DOG

Vet performs full health check

By law, if a puppy is not healthy at purchase, you are entitled to a refund or a replacement. Be sure to make an examination conditional to the purchase; your vet can look for signs of infectious diseases and parasites, and check the puppy's general state of health. The breeder will be asked to provide documents to verify that the puppy's parents are free from a variety of hereditary disorders. Apply similar conditions when acquiring an adult dog.

AVOID PUPPY FARMS

It is advisable, whenever possible, to buy your dog directly from a reputable breeder. Avoid puppy farms or mills, as they often provide inhumane conditions for mothers and give little attention to the puppies' health. Some newspaper advertisements are fronts for puppy farms; be suspicious if you visit a private address and cannot see the litter's mother. Also be wary of some pet shops – they can sometimes be fertile environments for a range of infectious diseases, and may supply you with an unhealthy individual purchased from a puppy farm.

YOUR NEW PUPPY

THE BEST AGE for a Golden Retriever puppy to leave its mother and enter your home is at about eight weeks old; puppies over 12 weeks old may already have formed unwanted habits. Make a careful choice after viewing several litters and prepare your home for the new arrival.

CHOOSING THE RIGHT PUPPY

VISITING A LITTER

Each puppy within a litter has its own unique personality. Those that boldly come forward to greet you are the most confident, while those that retire to the corners may just be tired, but could be shy. Decide which sex you prefer, then choose a healthy puppy that seems to have the character you are looking for.

Hold front paws closely together

THE ONE FOR YOU?

Golden Retriever puppies feel firm and surprisingly heavy. To ensure safe handling, support the puppy under its hindquarters when you examine it. Ask to see all documents concerning the parents' registration and freedom from inherited conditions such as eye diseases and hip dysplasia. Once you are happy with the litter's health and background, your final decision will rest ultimately on a particular puppy's looks and its endearing behaviour.

MEET THE PARENTS

Responsible breeders are proud of their breeding stock and will be delighted to introduce you to the litter's mother and also the father if he is available. Some may also show you all the other close relatives! The parents' appearance and behaviour will give some idea of the puppy's probable mature size and likely temperament. Do not buy a puppy from individuals who are unable to show you the mother; they may not be genuine breeders but agents for puppy farms. All reputable breeders will also permit you to return a puppy immediately if your vet feels there is good reason to do so.

SETTLING IN AT HOME

AN INVITING NEW HOME

When you arrive home with your new puppy, give it time to investigate its new environment. Line its crate with newspaper and soft bedding, and make it inviting by placing a food treat or toys inside. Leave the door open so the puppy can wander in and out at leisure. Your puppy will eventually view the crate as a comfortable sanctuary.

FIRST NIGHT ALONE

Your puppy's first night away from the security of its mother and litter is likely to be its most difficult. Provide a chewable toy for comfort and, if possible, place the crate in your bedroom to help reassure the puppy with your presence. It will cry, but do not respond – you will be unwittingly training it to cry for attention. For the first few weeks, set your alarm so you can get up in the night to take your puppy to relieve itself.

Puppy is distressed and tries to climb out of crate

SETTLING IN

With a little perseverance, your puppy will settle down and sleep. Furnish the crate with bedding, water, and newspaper for soiling so that the your puppy can remain safely inside. In time, it should accept sleeping outside your bedroom.

Resident dog investigates new arrival

EARLY TRAINING

GOLDEN RETRIEVER PUPPIES are quick learners, showing a strong desire to please. Once your puppy has moved in, begin gentle training for obedience and hygiene, rewarding all good behaviour. Encourage play with stimulating toys and arrange for regular contact with other dogs.

LEARNING WITH REWARDS

VERBAL PRAISE

Your genuine pleasure is readily expressed through enthusiastic words of approval and welcoming body posture. Goldens are eager pupils who are very sensitive to mannerisms and tone of voice; they learn quickly when verbally rewarded for good behaviour. Praise is very important; always use it in conjunction with food or stroke rewards.

Owner strokes along puppy's back. Avoid the head, which can be threatening

STROKING REWARD

Touch can act as a powerful training tool. Your puppy will instinctively ask to be stroked, but do not comply on demand. Only pet in response to good conduct, so that obedience is associated with desired physical attention.

ACQUIRING SOCIAL SKILLS

The first three months of your puppy's life represent its greatest learning period. If denied regular, ongoing contact with other dogs at this important time, your Golden may not develop the social skills necessary for mixing with new company. If you do not have another dog, ask your vet to help you organize weekly "puppy parties" to encourage natural, friendly interaction with other healthy puppies.

Puppy waits obediently

Edible rewards work well with most Goldens

FOOD TREAT

Golden Retrievers simply adore food. To exploit this breed characteristic sensibly, give tasty, low-calorie treats such as vitamin tablets as primary rewards and reinforce your pleasure with exuberant praise.

TOYS FOR YOUR NEW PUPPY

Jaw muscles are exercised through prolonged gnawing on chewable toy

SUITABLE TOYS FOR CHEWING AND PLAYING

Your puppy will love toys with a distinctive odour, and ones that are fun to chase, retrieve, or chew. Playing with them will stimulate your puppy both mentally and physically, but be careful with squeaky toys – some over-zealous Goldens accidentally swallow the "squeakers". All toys belong to you, so put them away when playtime is over.

TOYS AS REWARD AND COMFORT

Maintain your puppy's interest in a toy by limiting access to special circumstances only, such as periods alone in its crate, when the item will act as a soothing distraction. Keep a maximum of three distinctive toys. Toys given selectively as recognition of good conduct are exciting rewards, while those left lying around soon become boring.

HOUSE TRAINING INDOORS AND OUT

PAPER TRAINING

When your puppy puts its nose down and sniffs it usually signifies a desire to eliminate. Peak times for this are just after waking, eating, drinking, and exercise, so be prepared to quickly place your puppy on newspaper, and praise it when it urinates or messes. It is pointless to punish "accidents", but if you catch your puppy in the act, sternly say "No" to teach it that the paper must be used.

Puppy knows it has done well when it hears "Good dog!"

MOVING OUTSIDE

Begin outdoor training as soon as possible. Three-month-old Golden puppies need to empty their bladders about once every four hours. Take a small piece of soiled paper with you; the puppy will smell its own scent and be encouraged to transfer toileting outside. As it eliminates, say "Hurry up"; this will train your dog to relieve itself on that command.

INTRODUCING OUTDOORS

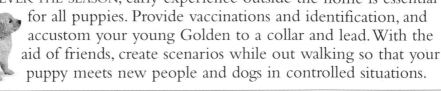

WHATEVER THE SEASON, early experience outside the home is essential for all puppies. Provide vaccinations and identification, and accustom your young Golden to a collar and lead. With the aid of friends, create scenarios while out walking so that your puppy meets new people and dogs in controlled situations.

IDENTIFICATION

STANDARD NAME TAG
Engraved or canister tags carry vital information about your dog, including a contact telephone number. When possible, also list your vet's emergency telephone number. A dab of nail varnish will prevent metal canisters from unscrewing.

Registration number is stored in this tiny microchip

PERMANENT METHODS
A tiny microchip, encased in glass, permanently stores important data. Inserted just under the skin on the neck, it provides safe and secure information that can be "read" using a hand-held scanner. Painless tattoos are another permanent alternative that might be available in your area.

INTRODUCTION TO COLLAR AND LEAD

1 Collar and lead training can begin indoors or outside as soon as you acquire your puppy. Start by letting the dog see and smell the collar. Then, avoiding eye contact, kneel down and put the collar on, distracting your puppy with words of encouragement. Reward your puppy's compliance with treats, physical contact, and praise. Actively play for a while, then take the collar off. Your puppy will soon learn to associate the collar with rewards, and should accept it without reluctance.

Put on a light, comfortable collar, distracting puppy with words, or using a treat or toy

2 Once your puppy is content wearing its collar, kneel down and attach a lead. Keeping the lead slack, entice your dog to one side with a toy or food reward, and as it moves towards the item, apply light tension to the lead. Offer your puppy the toy or treat, while giving it lavish praise.

Access to toy is reward for accepting lead

MEETING STRANGERS

Stage a planned meeting with a dog-loving friend while outside with your puppy. Ask your friend to kneel down to greet the puppy; this will help curb its inclination to jump up. Also, discourage direct eye contact, which can evoke an exaggerated submissive response – not uncommon in very young dogs. Finally, provide your friend with your puppy's favourite food treat to give as a reward for relatively calm behaviour.

Puppy happily accepts petting and reward from unfamiliar person

ESSENTIAL PUPPY INOCULATIONS

Your veterinarian will vaccinate your new puppy against a range of infectious diseases, and for additional protection may advise avoidance of unfamiliar dogs for a few weeks. Contact with known healthy dogs should continue, however, to ensure that your puppy becomes properly socialized.

ENCOUNTERING OTHER DOGS

Arrange for a friend with a placid dog to meet you on a walk. Ask your friend to instruct her dog to sit as you approach, and reward your puppy's calm response with treats and praise. Through routine meetings, your puppy learns that there is no need to jump on any animal that reminds it of its mother. In conjunction with this, regular interaction with puppies of a similar age should help develop desirable social skills.

Always walk your puppy on a lead for safe control

Socialized dog accepts puppy's presence with ease

DISCOURAGE JUMPING UP

Goldens enjoy life, and in their exuberance many tend to jump up onto people by way of a greeting. Do not encourage this annoying habit by slapping your thighs when calling your dog, and ask others to get down to puppy level during meetings to dissuade jumping up.

FIRST ROUTINES

EVEN WHEN YOU are not teaching it, a Golden puppy is learning about life. From the moment it enters your home, train your puppy to accept being left alone, to learn about permitted behaviour, and to come when called. Make sure all early experiences are good ones – they set patterns for life.

ACCEPTING BEING LEFT ALONE

No matter how much you enjoy being with your new puppy, there will be times when you must leave it on its own. Train your Golden to accept that this is part of its routine by confining it to its crate with an interesting reward, such as a hollow toy filled with a little peanut butter. Then quietly walk away, signalling "Wait". Gradually accustom your dog to being left alone for extended periods.

Crate must be equipped with fresh water and chewable toy for diversion

Owner walks away, giving hand signal that puppy will soon learn means "Wait"

STOP OVER-AGGRESSIVE PLAY

If one puppy hurts another during rough play, the wounded puppy will usually bite back or retire from the game. Either way, the aggressive dog learns a lesson. Do the same with your puppy. If it behaves unacceptably, say "No!" and stop play for a minute. If necessary, you may grab the scruff of the neck as a firm but painless admonition.

SEVERAL PUPPIES?

Any training requires the undivided attention of both you and your puppy. If you have two or more puppies, train just one at a time, keeping the others out of sight and beyond hearing distance. Otherwise, they may actually learn not to respond to your commands since their obedience is not being reinforced. Training sessions with individual puppies should only last for a maximum of 10 minutes. Afterwards, reward your puppy with plenty of exaggerated praise so that it can see your pleasure.

COMING TO YOU ON COMMAND

1 Your dog's safety depends on you. Central to all training is its responsiveness in coming to you on command. Having taught your puppy to accept a collar and lead, put these on the puppy and kneel a short distance away, with the lead tucked securely under one knee. Then hold an exciting toy which will be the reward for compliance.

Puppy is distracted and ignores owner

Distinctive or scented toy is appealing reward

2 Call your puppy's name in a clear, friendly tone to attract its attention. When it turns its head towards you, give the command "Come", and wave the toy as an enticement. Keep the lead slack; do not reel in your puppy but encourage it to come willingly towards you for the reward.

Owner repeats command, "Come"

When called, puppy turns around and sees toy

3 Welcome your puppy with open arms. Out of curiosity, it should walk towards you. As it moves, say "Good dog" in an enthusiastic voice. When the puppy reaches you, reward it with the toy. Never call your puppy to discipline it, or it will then associate returning to you with being reprimanded. Develop a happy bond so your puppy comes because it wants to be with you.

Intrigued puppy is now alert and eager to obey command

Words of approval and inviting gesture elicit response

COME, SIT, DOWN, STAY

TEACHING YOUR GOLDEN RETRIEVER puppy to understand basic obedience commands is easy. This is because it is among the most trainable of all breeds, and responds well to food rewards. Start training early, incorporating it into play sessions, to ensure that your puppy will always obey you.

COME AND SIT

1 Start training in a quiet, narrow space such as a hallway, preferably just before mealtime. Holding the puppy on a loose lead, briskly and cheerfully call its name and let it see that you have a food treat in your hand. As it starts to move towards you, give the command "Come". If there is no reaction, you may need to bend down, so that your puppy can clearly see the treat. Try to be enthusiastic, and while your puppy walks towards you, praise it by saying "Good dog".

2 As your puppy reaches you, move the treat above its head. To keep its eye on the food, your puppy will naturally sit. As it does so, issue the command "Sit" and immediately give the reward. Repeat the exercise regularly before each meal, when your puppy is attentive and will respond well to food incentives.

Tail held out shows puppy is not anxious or frightened

Puppy stretches along floor to receive edible prize

THE VALUE OF "NO!"

It is vital for everyone's well-being that your puppy quickly understands the meaning of "No!". With this one word, you can regain control and even prevent an accident. Just as you use a friendly voice and warm body language to reward, adopt a stern tone and a dominant stance when issuing this reprimand. There is no need to shout; once they know what behaviour you want, most Goldens are very eager to please. Nevertheless, it is best to practise all basic obedience commands indoors before moving outside, where your dog will be more easily diverted.

FOLLOW DOWN

1 Seat your puppy, then kneel beside it, securing the lead under one knee. Holding its collar with one hand, place a treat by its nose. If your puppy tries to get up, tuck its hindquarters under with your free hand and say "Sit". If it lunges for the food, try a squeaky toy.

2 Move the treat both forwards and down in an arc shape; your puppy should follow the movement with its nose. As it starts to lie down, give the command "Down". If your puppy refuses, gently raise the front legs into a begging position, then lower it down, rewarding its compliance with praise.

3 Maintaining your hold on the collar, move the food treat down to ground level until your puppy is lying flat. While it is in this position, reward your puppy with the treat and praise. Avoid too much praise because it can overexcite, causing the puppy to jump up and lick you.

Keep reward visible but held firmly until given

STAY DOWN

Having positioned your puppy down, give the command "Stay". With the lead held loosely in your hand, and maintaining eye contact, get up and walk in front, repeating "Stay". Use a raised palm gesture rather than food rewards; this will become a learned visual signal. Response to the "Stay" command is very important in potentially hazardous situations.

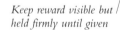

Puppy hears "Good dog" and knows owner is pleased

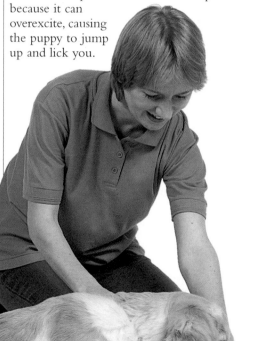

WALKING TO HEEL

A WELL-BEHAVED Golden Retriever walking obediently to heel is the perfect advertisement for this marvellous breed. The Golden's desire to please makes it a pleasure to train, therefore you can start indoor training without a lead from an early age and then graduate to lead training.

WALKING TO HEEL WITHOUT A LEAD

1 Kneel down to the right side of your seated puppy, taking hold of its collar with your left hand. Speak its name while showing a tasty food treat to attract and keep its attention.

Puppy smells potential reward

2 Hold the treat in front of the puppy's nose and walk in a straight line, while giving the command "Heel". The food scent will induce the puppy to follow. Keep your left hand low, ready to grasp the collar if the puppy tries to wander. When you stop walking, command "Wait".

3 Keeping the treat low to prevent jumping up, bend your knees and turn right, drawing the food around as you move. Repeat the command "Heel". Your puppy will speed up to walk around you and to keep up with the treat.

Front paws cross over as puppy turns to the right

4 With your puppy still to your left, hold the collar in your left hand, commanding "Steady". Place the treat near your puppy's mouth, then move it to the left. The puppy will follow. Train regularly, but only for a few minutes each time, finishing off with the treat.

Treat is moved left and puppy follows

HEELWORK WITH A LEAD

1 When your puppy is relaxed but alert, begin heelwork again with a long training lead. With your puppy to your left, hold the lead and a food treat in your right hand, and pick up the slack of the lead with your left. Gain your puppy's attention and command it to "Sit".

Owner repeats encouraging words

2 Move forwards on your left foot while giving the command "Heel". If your puppy walks too far ahead, give the lead a light jerk.

3 With the puppy beside you in the heel position, offer it the reward and say "Good dog". Repeat "Sit" and praise it when it obeys.

5 Once the right turn has been mastered, begin left-turn training. Hold the treat above the puppy's nose to slow it down, while speeding up your own circling movement to the left. Keep the puppy close, controlling it with the lead, and command "Steady" as it follows you around.

4 After learning to walk in a straight line to the "Heel" command, teach your puppy to turn to the right by guiding it with the treat. Only train for short periods to maintain interest.

Puppy concentrates intently on food reward, following its every movement

INDOOR TRAINING

YOUR GOLDEN RETRIEVER will treat your home as its own personal territory. Much of its life will be spent indoors, so make sure it understands that you set and enforce the rules. Teach your Golden to wait for you to initiate activity, and to go willingly to its bed when you decide playtime is over.

SPENDING QUALITY TIME TOGETHER

Dog gives owner brightly coloured toy as part of the game

Set aside time each day to offer your Golden some indoor physical and mental activity. This not only strengthens the bond between you and your dog, but reinforces basic obedience training. Try to devise different types of games to stimulate certain areas of behaviour. For example, play that involves fetching and relinquishing a favourite toy is an enjoyable way of teaching your Golden not to be possessive. It is also important to vary the time of play, or your dog will learn to expect a particular activity at a given time.

FOLLOW SIMPLE RETRAINING RULES

Remember all the principles of basic training, and always return to them if behavioural problems develop in adulthood. When your Golden understands simple obedience – to come, sit, lie down, and stay – virtually all undesirable behaviour can be corrected. Golden Retrievers are more trainable than many other dog breeds, and have a good but limited ability to understand language. Try not to overload your dog with information; use short, sharp words, and issue commands only if you know that you can enforce them.

WAITING PATIENTLY

All dogs enjoy attention and will constantly ask for it unless taught not to. As pack leader, it is you, not your Golden, who decides where and when to initiate activity. Provide your dog with a bed or crate – a personal area to regard as its own. It will learn to retire there happily while you are relaxing, or otherwise engaged.

ACCEPTING STRANGERS

Golden Retrievers enjoy receiving visitors – sometimes too much! Ensure that your dog is not a nuisance by training it to sit when a guest arrives. This eliminates its tendency to become overexcited and discourages any territorial guarding, inherent in some males. To reinforce this calm behaviour, ask your visitor to disregard your dog at first. Always reward good behaviour with praise, a gentle stroke, or a favourite treat.

Obedient Golden sits close to owner

Owner exaggerates words and actions to convey displeasure

UNDERSTANDING WHAT IS WRONG

Adopt assertive body language and a stern voice to admonish your dog when it breaks certain rules, such as climbing onto forbidden furniture. Whenever possible, reprimand bad behaviour at once. If you wait until after the event, your dog will only understand your anger, not the reason behind it.

RELINQUISHING A COVETED ITEM

The Golden's most common unwanted behaviour is guarding food or possessions. To prevent this from becoming a problem, train your dog, using food rewards, to drop and surrender all objects on demand. Some Goldens may display possessive tendencies towards certain toys. When you finish playing, make a point of putting away all toys. This makes them more desirable to your dog, and therefore more useful as a control tool.

OUTSIDE THE HOME

ALTHOUGH IT IS ESSENTIAL for your Golden Retriever to exercise outdoors, there are all kinds of potential dangers that can put your dog at risk and affect the safety of others. To uphold your social obligations and keep your pet from being a nuisance, contain it in a healthy, hazard-free environment.

SHELTER AND EXERCISE

COMFORTABLE OUTDOOR KENNEL
If you plan to house your dog in a kennel, familiarize it from an early age. Provide a solid, well-insulated, chew-proof kennel that will become your dog's cosy sanctuary. Never leave your dog kennelled alone for long periods; canines need social contact.

CLEAN, SPACIOUS RUN
A hygienic run attached to the kennel is ideal for several dogs, providing fresh air and limited exercise. However, this is not an alternative to supervised walks. Golden Retrievers have large energy reserves and are prone to weight gain unless they are allowed physical activity outside their runs.

CONTROL OUTDOORS

HALF-CHECK COLLAR
Fit a half-check collar as a handling control. The soft webbing should lie around your dog's throat, while the chain sits on the back of its neck. A tug on the lead will tighten the collar without causing pain.

HEAD HALTER
Headstrong characters respond best to a head halter. At rest, this fits loosely over the muzzle, allowing the jaws to open. If your dog pulls forward, its impetus tightens the halter, pulls the head down, and closes the jaws.

MUZZLE
In extreme cases, fit a muzzle to obey local laws or to prevent your dog from scavenging. Use the basket variety in the appropriate size, which will permit panting and barking. Do not leave a muzzled dog unattended for long periods.

HAND-FREE CONTROL

As Golden Retrievers are such an obedient breed, they respond well to "hands-off" lead training. Secure the lead handle through your belt, then walk, stop, and walk again in a variety of directions. Your dog will quickly learn to accompany you – mirroring your every move – and will not pull against you when it sees that your hands are free.

ALWAYS GIVE PROMPT DISCIPLINE

Golden Retrievers are lively, inquisitive dogs that left unsupervised, may investigate further than you would like. If your dog has engaged in destructive digging, for example, reprimand it at once so that it understands why you are displeased. Enforce a lie-down and stop all play;

if you are away from home, return at once. Young male Goldens in particular may need obedience reinforced when they are outdoors.

PLANNING A SAFE AND SECURE GARDEN

The greatest hazard presented by your garden is the risk of escape. Check that all fencing is sturdy, gate latches secure, and that hedges have no gaps. Install wire mesh where necessary. Keep all garden chemicals safely locked away, and if you have outdoor lighting, ensure that no cables are exposed – they may be chewed. To prevent damage to your lawn, train your dog to use a specific site as its toilet. Be certain to store all waste and any horticultural tools securely out of reach, and do not establish plants that may be poisonous to dogs. Always watch your Golden carefully near a lit barbecue to ensure that it does not lick hot implements, and cover ornamental ponds.

Housing for rubbish bins

Wire mesh beneath locked gate

Sturdy fencing

Compost contained in bin

Garden chemicals stored in greenhouse

Sand-pit toilet

Non-toxic plants

Fenced-in vegetable garden

Plant pots tied together for stability

Covered pond

Lit barbecue must be supervised

Enclosed dog house

TRAVEL AND BOARDING

WITH TIME AND EXPERIENCE, your Golden should happily accept both travelling with you and being left behind. Introduce car journeys as early as possible, making them safe and enjoyable. Whenever you visit a new area, supervise your Golden's behaviour to ensure its safety, and that of others.

HOLIDAYS WITH OR WITHOUT YOUR DOG

DOG-SITTING SERVICES
Dog-sitting services are a good alternative to kennels, especially in urban areas. Ask friends or your vet to recommend a reliable agency that can supply a Golden-loving carer to look after your dog and your home while you are away. Always leave dog-sitters with a list of routine instructions, emergency telephone numbers, and general house rules.

QUALITY BOARDING KENNELS
Before kennelling your Golden, visit a few establishments first to decide which one you are happiest with. If you intend to board your dog regularly, introduce it to kennels early in life so that it learns to enjoy all return visits.

PREPARING FOR A TRIP
Most Goldens are quiet travellers and willing to go almost anywhere. If your Golden is coming with you on a trip, remember to pack its food and water bowls, collar, lead, and bedding – your dog may even enjoy carrying a few items itself! It is also advisable to add holiday contact addresses or telephone numbers to its name tag, and to ensure that all inoculations are up to date. Once there, locate a local vet who can deal with any emergencies.

Purpose-made rucksack allows dog to carry its own light load

SAFE TRAVELLING BY CAR

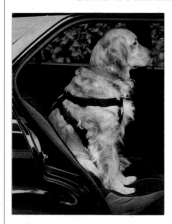

CANINE SEATBELT

Any passenger is at risk of injury in the event of a car accident, but an unrestrained one may also cause injury to others. Secure your dog on all journeys with a special canine seatbelt. This is like a child's harness, which attaches to the standard seatbelt anchors. With this device, your dog is kept reassuringly in place, so that it cannot distract the driver.

HOT CARS ARE DEATHTRAPS

Heatstroke is one of the most common causes of preventable death in dogs. A dog cannot sweat other than through its pads, so excess body heat can only be reduced through panting. In hot conditions, the body temperature rises quickly, sometimes within minutes, and if there is no escape a dog can die. Never leave your dog in your car in warm or sunny weather, even parked in the shade or with the windows slightly open.

REAR-LOADED CRATE

If you own a hatchback vehicle, you can transport your Golden in its crate. This way, your dog is contained and your car is kept free from dog hair or chewing damage. Introduce your Golden to its crate during puppyhood, as its regular bed and playpen in the home. Then, when the crate is used as transport, your dog will be inclined to relax and enjoy the journey. Alternatively, restrict your dog to the back of an estate car fitted with a sturdy, purpose-made dog grille. On long trips, stop every few hours to allow your dog to exercise, drink, and relieve itself.

Each dog is accommodated in its individual container

BE CONSIDERATE OF OTHERS

Many places have specific dog-control regulations, so look out for them wherever you are. Observe all signs, and keep your Golden controlled on a lead, especially in designated areas such as parks and on beaches. Just as you would at home, always clean up after your dog. Carry a supply of plastic bags, or use a "poop scoop", and deposit mess in special waste bins if available. Never let your Golden be a nuisance to others.

CONSTRUCTIVE PLAY

GOLDEN RETRIEVERS NEED mental stimulation as well as physical exercise. Satisfy both needs by creating activities that utilize the breed's special abilities; games involving retrieving will be especially rewarding. Use playtime to reinforce basic training, to strengthen your bond as owner, and simply to have fun.

Golden naturally holds glove without dropping it

"SPEAK" AND "HUSH"

Although excessive barking is not usually a problem associated with Goldens, it is still useful to have control over this canine trait. Train your dog, using food or toy rewards, to bark on the "Speak" command, and to be quiet when it sees you put a finger to your lips and say "Hush". This is useful to enforce household peace and to encourage watchdog barking.

RETRIEVING ON DEMAND

Put your Golden's retrieving abilities to use by training it to fetch an item such as a gardening glove. Start by placing the glove in your dog's mouth and repeat "Hold". Complete the exercise by throwing the glove, and commanding "Fetch", followed by "Come". Initially use a lead, so your Golden Retriever knows you want it to return, rather than just play with, the item.

FOLLOWING A SCENT TRAIL

Show your Golden a toy with a distinctive odour, then secretly hide it out of sight. Command your dog to "Find", and use an encouraging tone of voice as it gets nearer, or a dull one if it goes off track. To progress outdoors, sprinkle a line of aniseed to lay a scent trail, with a toy at the end as the reward.

HAVING FUN WITH MOVING OBJECTS

Goldens can develop limited soccer skills, although they lack the desire to win that some terriers have! Giving words of encouragement, teach your dog to roll a ball with its nose. Avoid using food rewards as they can be too potent a distraction from the game.

A dog can become skilful at pushing a ball with its nose

Dog recognizes your authority by giving paw

GAME OF "HIGH FIVE"

The human greeting known as "high five" is actually a submissive gesture in canine terms. By training your Golden to sit and offer its paw, you will help reinforce your role as natural pack leader. It is often beneficial to encourage children to play this game, so that your dog soon learns they too are in command.

EAGER TO WORK

Channel your Golden's inborn desire to serve and retrieve by providing it with something useful to do. Fetching the newspaper or carrying a light load of shopping can be psychologically rewarding for your Golden, but distracting food and toy treats should be avoided. However, offering verbal praise will encourage your dog to undertake these tasks, while fulfilling its need for mental and physical activity.

Basket is carefully delivered with contents intact

END PLAYING WITH REWARDS AND PRAISE

Specially devised games will keep your dog's mind busy and alert. Adequate mental as well as physical exercise can help reduce the incidence of boredom-related problems, such as chewing furniture or excessive self-grooming. It is easy to incorporate training into play by continually reinforcing basic obedience commands such as "Sit", "Stay", "Come", and "Down", and by rewarding good behaviour. Always finish games on a positive note, with food treats, stroking, or encouraging words, so that your Golden looks forward to future activities. Just as with children, if learning is fun, dogs will want to learn more.

GOOD CONTROL

YOU WILL FIND THAT THE Golden Retriever is among the most obedient and family-oriented of all the dog breeds. Nevertheless, unacceptable behavioural problems can develop, many of which arise from natural instincts. Most difficulties can be prevented through proper care and early training.

HAPPILY OCCUPIED ALONE

When left alone, some dogs become anxious, and occasionally destructive. Exercise your dog before you go out and always leave and return without a fuss. To distract it, give your dog a beef bone, or a toy with a hollow centre filled with a food spread.

Lead ensures control for first meeting

FRIENDLY CANINE MEETINGS

It is possible to socialize your Golden Retriever through planned meetings with a well-controlled dog. If your Golden is fearful or aggressive, initially keep both dogs apart, then gradually draw them nearer as your dog relaxes. Let them investigate and play together, rewarding your dog's composed response, but stopping all games if it behaves badly. At the first signs of nervousness or hostility, turn your dog's head away and produce a favourite toy as a distraction. After several meetings, your dog will naturally show curious interest, not apprehension, when meeting new dogs.

LEARNING TO RESIST TEMPTATION

Prevent begging by never giving your Golden food while you are eating; the occasional titbit will encourage this annoying habit more than regular offerings. If your dog begs, command it to lie down, then look away. When you have finished eating, reward your Golden's obedience with play and praise, not food treats.

Girl avoids eye contact while eating ice cream

*Golden is alert
but relaxed in
presence of
opened umbrella*

*Umbrella
can appear
threatening*

ACCEPTING NEW SITUATIONS

If your Golden Retriever is frightened by a new sight or sound, reintroduce the stimulus when the dog is far enough away that it is not provoked. Over time, reduce the distance between your dog and the distressing situation, always rewarding calm acceptance. Eventually, your Golden will learn that there is no cause for concern.

DETERRENTS FOR CHEWING

Young, bored Goldens can be dramatically destructive, usually when left unsupervised. Make an object that is likely to be chewed less enticing by spraying it with a safe but bitter-tasting aerosol. When the dog investigates the object, the taste should deter any further interest in chewing. Trainers call this aversion therapy.

*Spray liberally
on objects that
you do not
want chewed*

*Owner maintains
physical as well
as verbal control*

*Golden is offered
food treat for good
behaviour, and
takes it carefully*

MEETING STRANGERS

Goldens can be flamboyantly friendly, but not all strangers appreciate wet licks! If your dog is over-zealous, keep it on a lead so that you are able to control it when visitors arrive. As the guest enters, command your Golden to "Sit" and "Stay". To elicit an acceptable welcome, ask the guest to crouch down and avoid eye contact, while giving your dog a food treat.

FOODS FOR YOUR DOG

GENERALLY, THE GOLDEN RETRIEVER is a voracious eater; if it refuses to eat, it is time to call your vet. There is a wide, sophisticated choice of commercially produced dog foods to cater for all ages and dietary needs. Alternatively, feed your Golden a selection of nutritious, home-prepared meals.

CANNED FOODS

At one time, canned food was the most popular diet for many dogs. These moist, meaty diets come in a wide variety of flavours and textures to satisfy your Golden's large appetite. High in protein, they are usually mixed with dry dog meal to add calories and carbohydrates, although some are nutritionally complete on their own.

Standard variety

Special formula for clinical conditions

"Stew" with gravy

Chunks in jelly

DRY MEAL

Crunchy dry meal is added to canned food to improve the texture, contribute fibre and fat, as well as exercise the jaws.

COMPLETE DRY FOODS

Nutritionally balanced, complete dry foods are a practical way to feed your Golden. Concentrated, they contain about four times the calories of canned foods, so a dog needs smaller amounts. It can be stored in bulk, and there are varieties to suit all ages and for specific medical conditions, such as bowel inflammation or impaired kidney function.

HIGH-ENERGY
Puppies require nutrient-rich, easily-digestible foods to sustain growth.

REGULAR
Adult formulas maintain mature dogs on a variety of activity levels.

LOW-CALORIE
Older, overweight, or sedentary dogs need less energy from their food.

TEETH-CLEANING
These large, crunchy chunks promote healthy gums and help control tartar.

SEMI-MOIST FOODS

These foods are packaged in many flavours, even cheese, and have three times the calories of canned foods. A high carbohydrate content makes semi-moist foods unsuitable for diabetic dogs. Like dry foods, they can be left out all day to be eaten at leisure – a situation that seldom arises with Goldens!

SUITABLE CHEWS

Large, hard chews that work teeth and massage the gums are suitable for Goldens. Take care with small chews that may be easily swallowed, or sterilized bones, which can break teeth.

Rawhide chew

TREATS AND BISCUITS

You may enjoy giving your dog food treats, but remember that many are highly calorific, which can lead to obesity. Offer snacks as rewards, not on demand, giving a fixed daily quota. The more treats your Golden receives, the smaller its regular meals should be.

MIXED ASSORTMENT   MARROWBONE   BEEF BONE SHAPES   CHEESE-FLAVOURED

TABLE FOODS

In general, a diet that is well-balanced for us is also nourishing for canines. Never allow begging by feeding your dog "table scraps". Instead, prepare it a special portion made up of equal parts meat and vegetables, rice, or pasta. Spices can cause digestive upsets.

Chicken is easily digested and lower in calories than red meat

Rice adds bulk and energy-giving carbohydrate to the meal

PRESCRIPTION DIETS

Medical conditions such as heart disease, allergies, and obesity require a special diet as part of the treatment. There are various canned prescription foods available, and your vet can advise which is best for your dog.

Mix of bite-sized pieces is ideal for a convalescing diet

Prescription diets are nutritionally formulated to aid recovery

HEALTHY EATING

PROVIDE YOUR GOLDEN RETRIEVER with nutritious meals, in quantities appropriate to its age and energy requirements, and remember to supply plenty of fresh water to avoid dehydration. Since most Goldens love food – and will overeat if allowed – prevent begging or obesity by feeding at set times.

DIETARY NEEDS FOR ALL AGES

Always serve food at room temperature

GROWING PUPPY
Feed your puppy four equal portions of complete dry puppy food daily. If preferred, offer two cereal and milk meals, and two of home-made or canned food. Eliminate a cereal meal at three months and the other cereal meal at six months.

MATURE ADULT
Health, activity levels, personal metabolism, and neutering are all factors that can affect an adult dog's nutritional requirements. Feed your Golden twice daily, but refer any excessive weight gain to your veterinarian.

WAITING FOR FOOD

Without proper training, Goldens are inclined to beg shamelessly for food, especially for titbits while you are eating. To prevent this, establish a set routine for its mealtimes, only offering your dog food in its own bowl. Teach your dog to sit and wait in the presence of food and to eat only when released to do so.

Owner's hand signal and "Stay" command teach Golden self-restraint

ELDERLY GOLDEN
Older dogs have reduced energy demands and should be fed smaller portions of low-calorie, quality foods. This should help prevent obesity, which puts undue strain on internal organs and the hind legs.

DAILY ENERGY DEMANDS FOR ALL STAGES OF LIFE					
AGE	WEIGHT	CALORIES	DRY FOOD	SEMI-MOIST	CANNED/MEAL
2 MONTHS	5 kg (11 lb)	1,120	335 g (12 oz)	380 g (13 oz)	555 g/190 g (20 oz/7 oz)
3 MONTHS	10 kg (22 lb)	1,645	480 g (17 oz)	530 g (19 oz)	825 g/285 g (29 oz/10 oz)
6 MONTHS	25 kg (55 lb)	2,325	700 g (25 oz)	765 g (27 oz)	1165 g/395 g (41 oz/14 oz)
TYPICAL ADULT	26–43 kg (57–95 lb)	1,265–1,850	380–555 g (13–20 oz)	425–630 g (15–22 oz)	630–925 g/215–300 g (22–33 oz/8–11 oz)
ACTIVE ADULT	26–43 kg (57–95 lb)	1,440–2,100	425–630 g (15–22 oz)	480–700 g (17–25 oz)	700–1050 g/265–380 g (25–37 oz/9–13 oz)
VERY ACTIVE ADULT	26–43 kg (57–95 lb)	2,015–2,940	595–880 g (21–31 oz)	670–980 g (24–35 oz)	1010–1470 g/335–500 g (36–52 oz/12–18 oz)
ELDERLY (10 YEARS+)	26–43 kg (57–95 lb)	1,150–1,680	335–500 g (12–18 oz)	385–555 g (14–20 oz)	555–840 g/190–285 g (20–30 oz/7–10 oz)

FEEDING REQUIREMENTS

These figures represent an approximate guide only. Remember that each dog has its own specific nutritional needs, and that different brands of food vary in calories.

Always provide a well-balanced diet to meet your dog's daily energy requirements. If you are uncertain of what is best for your Golden, seek detailed professional advice.

CHAMPION SCAVENGERS

Regardless of how much you feed your Golden, the temptation of scavenging for extra food is usually too good to miss. In the quest to seek and devour, your dog may accidently swallow inedible or damaging objects. Teach it from an early age to "Drop" articles on command. It is also wise to secure all rubbish, keeping tempting items out of reach. In severe cases, secure your dog with a muzzle.

Pedal bins are the perfect height for scavenging success

CONTROLLING AN UNSAVOURY APPETITE

Goldens have a rather unrefined palate, and may be attracted to the most repugnant refuse. Outdoors, they will quickly sniff out animal droppings, and regard them as dessert! This is natural behaviour, and horse, rabbit, or deer faeces can actually be nourishing for dogs. Eating canine droppings, however, may cause intestinal ailments. Tell your dog "No", and make it drop any excrement it picks up. A spice-treated stool is also a good deterrent.

BASIC BODY CARE

GOLDEN RETRIEVERS HAVE an excellent natural anatomy which requires minimal maintenance. However, wax can quickly build-up in its close-hanging ears, while its thick coat suffers from the wear and tear of rolling in mud. Check the cleanliness of all body openings on a daily basis.

ENSURING CLEAR, HEALTHY EYES

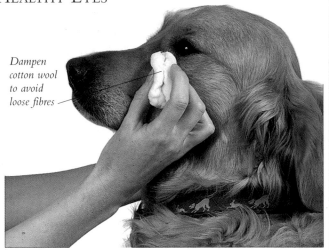

Healthy eyes are bright and sparkling with dull pink mucous membranes. Some older Goldens develop slightly droopy lower eyelids, in which debris can collect and cause inflammation. Bathe the area around your dog's eyes daily with cotton wool moistened with tepid salt water. If the eyes appear reddened or cloudy, or weep a yellow or green discharge, contact your vet to arrange an examination.

Dampen cotton wool to avoid loose fibres

BRUSHING THE TEETH

Firmly pull back lip to reveal teeth

Use specially-prepared canine toothpaste

Check daily for any debris lodged in the cheeks or roof of the mouth. Once a week, clean the teeth with a soft brush, working up and down to massage the gums. Avoid human toothpaste, which froths and can be swallowed.

PREVENT TARTAR

Without routine cleaning, tartar can accumulate on the teeth, leading to bad breath, infection, and gum disease. In addition to regular professional scaling, rawhide chews are helpful in controlling tartar build-up. This Golden's teeth and gums require medical attention.

INSPECTING THE EARS

When cleaning the ears, check carefully for wax, odour, inflammation, and foreign material such as grass seeds. Remove excess wax with a dampened tissue; a cotton bud can act like a plunger and push wax further into the ear.

WASHING THE PAWS

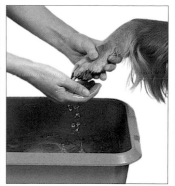

Mud can harden between the Golden's pads and in the feathering on the legs. Wash the dirty areas with tepid or cool water, continuously rubbing with your fingers to help remove all deposits. Only use cleansers safe for human skin. Rinse and dry the paws thoroughly afterwards.

CUTTING THE NAILS

Clip after bathing, when nails are soft and pliable

A Golden Retriever's nails seldom need clipping. If they do grow long, command your dog to sit and use a non-crushing "guillotine" clipper. Look for tan-coloured nails where the quick is visible to give you a guideline on how much to cut. Always reward your dog for good behaviour.

WHERE TO CLIP NAILS
The pink interior, called the quick or nail bed, contains blood vessels and nerves, but this cannot be seen in black nails. Always cut in front of the quick. If unsure, ask your vet.

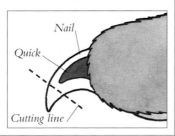

Nail

Quick

Cutting line

ANAL HYGIENE

Excessive licking or dragging of the rear can mean that the scent-producing anal sacs are blocked, causing discomfort. Wearing protective gloves, squeeze the sacs empty, applying firm pressure from both sides. Use absorbent material to collect the fluid.

MAINTAINING THE COAT

DAILY GROOMING AND OCCASIONAL bathing are essential to keep your Golden's lush coat healthy and attractive. More frequent bathing reduces the substances in dog dander, to which some people are allergic. During your dog's heavy moulting periods, grooming twice-daily is advisable.

ROUTINE GROOMING

REMOVING TANGLES
Using a slicker brush, remove dead hair and untangle mats in the feathering on the legs, chest, and tail. During moults, expect large amounts of fine down as well as the thicker top coat. Always check for signs of parasites or skin irritations.

DOUBLE-SIDED BRUSHING
A bristle brush is ideal for ridding the coat of dried-on debris. Be careful with the pin side; Goldens are prone to various skin infections which often originate from scratches.

MASSAGING THE SKIN
When all tangles, debris, and dead hair have been removed, massage your Golden's skin – it is both pleasurable for your dog and conditioning for its coat. Drawing a soft rubber "fingered" grooming device through the coat should stimulate production of the essential, natural oils that promote a glossy, healthy sheen.

Long strokes follow natural lay of hair

TIDYING THE PAWS
If the hair has grown too long on the paws, cut neatly around each foot and carefully between the toes with blunt-ended scissors. This will help prevent grass seeds and other unwanted materials from lodging painfully in the paws.

SHINING THE COAT

Complete the grooming routine by smoothing the entire coat with a clean, dry chamois leather. This wipes any loose flakes of skin from the surface and creates a brilliant shine. Let your dog know that grooming is complete by giving the release command "OK", then reward its obedience with praise or active play.

Most Goldens find grooming enjoyable

COMBING THE FEATHERS

Brush the feathery hair on the legs, chest, and tail, especially on long-coated Golden Retrievers. Use a comb to remove any remaining tangles and stray strands of hair.

BATHING YOUR DOG

1 Bathing cleans mud and grime from your dog and is useful for treating a variety of skin conditions, or simply to restore the coat's natural lustre. Keeping a firm grip on your dog and with a non-slip mat in the bath for safety, wash your dog thoroughly with dog or baby shampoo in tepid to warm water. Then carefully rinse off the lather, removing all deposits from under the legs and tail.

Avoid shampoo around the eyes, and clean face with a wet cloth

2 After rinsing, squeeze excess water from the coat and wrap your dog in a towel, while praising good behaviour. Let the dog shake, then rub dry or use a hairdryer set to warm, not hot. Only consider washing your dog outside when it can dry naturally in warm weather.

GROOMING AS A BASIC RITUAL

Grooming is comforting to most dogs, but some dominant individuals may resent it. To avoid future problems, introduce grooming routines as soon as you acquire your Golden, as part of standard obedience training. To help establish your leadership, command your puppy to lie down and lift its leg submissively before you begin grooming.

BASIC HEALTH

SINCE IT CANNOT tell you if something is wrong, you must pay special attention to your Golden Retriever's health. Observe how your dog moves and behaves; any changes in activity or regular habits may be warning signs of problems. Arrange annual health check-ups, and use your vet as a source of advice.

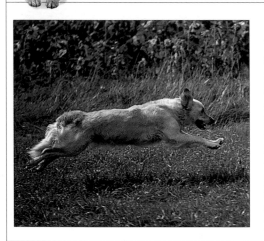

EASY, GRACEFUL MOVEMENT

Throughout life your Golden Retriever should walk, trot, and run in an easy, fluid manner. A cumbersome gait can be caused by excess weight, while difficulties lying down or getting up may portend joint problems – not uncommon, especially in older dogs. Limping is a sign that one leg in particular hurts, and head bobbing while walking is another indication of pain. Watch your dog during its daily activities and note any anomalies in behaviour. If you notice any discomfort or loss of mobility, take your dog to the vet for an examination.

SOUND APPETITE AND EATING HABITS

Your dog's early feeding and toilet routines are usually maintained throughout life. The Golden eats heartily and rarely experiences a loss in appetite, even when mildly ill; regard any drop in appetite as the sign of a potentially major problem. A heightened appetite without weight gain can indicate a thyroid problem; asking for food but then not eating it can mean tooth pain. Increased thirst is always significant and may be a sign of infection or conditions such as diabetes and liver or kidney disease. Any change in eating and

toileting habits should be reported to your veterinarian; seek medical advice if the consistency of your dog's stools changes from what you would normally expect.

Excessive drinking may be medically significant

MOOD CHANGES

Dogs are creatures of habit, so watch out for any changes in behaviour. If your Golden is reluctant to rise in the morning, shows little interest in play, or moves awkwardly, it could be ill. Age slows down all dogs, but so can some medical conditions such as poor circulation or neurological problems.

CARING FOR THE OLDER DOG

Be prepared for your dog to age. Like elderly people, old Goldens are less active and can become hard of hearing. Be patient with your dog's slow behaviour, and gentle in your handling. Accommodate these changes and try to create less physically demanding games. Mental stimulation is very important as it helps to delay the body's decline.

REGULAR HEALTH CHECKS

Vet uses stethoscope to monitor heart and lung sounds

Up-to-date vaccinations and annual health check-ups can increase your dog's longevity. Some treatable conditions, such as splenic tumours or liver disease, are not outwardly obvious but may be diagnosed upon physical examination. Problems discovered early are easier to treat. As your dog ages, your vet may recommend more detailed check-ups, including blood sampling, and may advise twice-yearly clinic visits.

MAKING VISITS TO THE VET FUN

Introduce your Golden Retriever to the veterinary clinic before it needs any treatment, so that it can have an investigative sniff and explore the premises. Ask your vet to give your dog a food treat while it is there, to make the next visit more appealing. If your vet does not supply treats, bring some with you and offer them when your dog is inoculated; this will provide suitable distraction from any unpleasantness. Repeat trips can be made less of a hardship for you, too, by taking out insurance on your pet's health. This will ensure that your dog can benefit from the most sophisticated diagnostics and treatments.

COMMON PROBLEMS

ALL DOGS ARE PRONE to internal and external parasites, and the Golden Retriever is no exception. Ear infections, as well as skin conditions, are common to the breed, as are excess chewing injuries and knee strains – especially in old, overweight Goldens.

COMMON PARASITES

Parasites are an occupational hazard, but many can be controlled with insecticides. Once indoors, always check your Golden's coat for signs of fleas, ticks, or mange, all of which cause skin irritation.

FLEA INFESTATION
This common parasite injects saliva when it bites, causing skin irritation and scratching. Use flea-control methods recommended by your vet.

INTERNAL PESTS
A dog's intestines, lungs, and heart can make ideal homes for worms. Visible signs include a poor coat and, common in puppies, a bloated abdomen.

TYPICAL CANINE COMPLAINTS

With any breed, most health problems are preventable. Prevention is always a preferable alternative to treatment. Inspect your dog's teeth and skin regularly – especially on the ears and between the toes – and update its vaccinations.

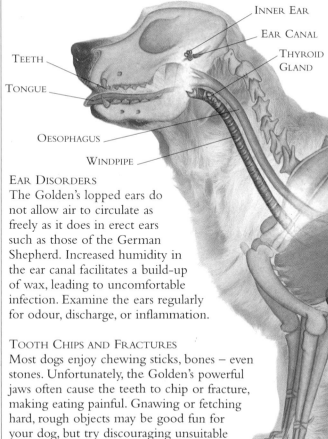

INNER EAR

EAR CANAL

THYROID GLAND

TEETH

TONGUE

OESOPHAGUS

WINDPIPE

EAR DISORDERS
The Golden's lopped ears do not allow air to circulate as freely as it does in erect ears such as those of the German Shepherd. Increased humidity in the ear canal facilitates a build-up of wax, leading to uncomfortable infection. Examine the ears regularly for odour, discharge, or inflammation.

TOOTH CHIPS AND FRACTURES
Most dogs enjoy chewing sticks, bones – even stones. Unfortunately, the Golden's powerful jaws often cause the teeth to chip or fracture, making eating painful. Gnawing or fetching hard, rough objects may be good fun for your dog, but try discouraging unsuitable play items to prevent dental damage or mouth lacerations and punctures.

Parasites are only one cause of itchy skin

OBVIOUS SIGNS OF DISCOMFORT

PERSISTENT LICKING
All dogs lick their skin to clean wounds and for general coat grooming, but obsessive licking of any part of the body can indicate a serious disorder. The Golden's anal sacs sometimes become blocked, which can lead to excessive licking.

Licking flank removes debris from fur

SCRATCHING
Dogs often scratch because of parasites, although allergies or injuries are causes too. In Goldens, scratching can lead to a high incidence of moist skin infection, called "hot spots". These unpleasant, pungent sores spread rapidly if left untreated.

LUNGS

STOMACH

SPLEEN

ADRENAL GLAND

KIDNEY

INTESTINES

JOINT DISEASE
Joints are vulnerable if a young dog carries too much weight during its growth phase. Hips, knees, hocks, and ankles can become inflamed, leading to painful arthritis.

BLADDER

ANAL SAC

LIVER

HEART

INTESTINAL PARASITES
Intestinal worms and other internal parasites such as *Giardia* and *Coccidia* may cause diarrhoea. Lung and heart worms reduce exercise tolerance, sometimes with vomiting and weight loss.

PAINFUL STRAINS
Endurance and agility are important attributes for any working dog. Your Golden's muscles, tendons, and ligaments are designed to support an active individual at optimum weight. Obesity often leads to injuries, as can over-vigorous exercise in normally sedentary dogs. A torn knee ligament is a serious injury most commonly found in older, overweight Golden Retrievers. Unfortunately, it is a complex condition requiring surgery.

BREED-SPECIFIC PROBLEMS

THROUGH SELECTIVE BREEDING for desirable traits, some potentially harmful genes are also pooled. Similar to other breeds, the Golden Retriever has its own variety of inherited medical problems. The most common conditions involve the joints, eyes, and intestines; obesity is an additional problem.

HIP DYSPLASIA

This hip joint condition is partly inherited and partly related to excessive weight, or over-strenuous activity during puppyhood. Signs of the condition are thigh muscle wasting and discomfort on rising. In severe cases, dogs "bunny hop" to diminish pain. A useful hip-testing scheme has been devised by veterinary associations and kennel clubs.

NORMAL HIPS
The hip is a basic ball-and-socket joint. In healthy hips such as these, the head (ball) of the femur sits comfortably and firmly in the acetabulum (socket) of the hip bone.

DYSPLASTIC JOINTS
This X-ray of a Golden with severe hip dysplasia shows shallow, rough hip sockets and abrasive femoral heads. Any movement of one against the other causes pain.

HEREDITARY EYE DISEASES

Golden Retrievers carry the risk of developing two inherited eye diseases that may eventually lead to blindness: cataracts and progressive retinal atrophy – a later-life condition where the retina "dies". Breeding stock should have their eyes routinely checked for damaged retinas or any irregularities. It will soon be possible through DNA blood "fingerprinting" to detect individual carriers of these diseases.

CLOUDING OF THE LENSES
This dog has sight-impairing cataracts. Although painless, the once-clear lenses have become crystalline and opaque. In some cases an operation can restore limited sight.

IMPORTANCE OF HEALTH SCREENING

All conscientious breeders participate in accredited screening programmes, often jointly run by kennel clubs and veterinary associations. They will be able to provide certificates stating that a dog is clear of inherited eye disorders, and give a comparative rating for any hip abnormalities. In a number of countries, anatomical, behavioural, and hereditary factor surveys are carried out by breed clubs, with dogs classified as "recommended for breeding", "suitable for breeding", or "not suitable".

OTHER DISORDERS COMMON IN GOLDENS

Although the Golden has a life expectancy of 13–15 years – longer than other breeds of a similar size – it is still susceptible to a number of inherited conditions. Prevention may be possible through careful breeding, but in cases when it is not, your vet can prescribe treatment and dietary advice. Obesity puts an extra strain on your Golden's constitution.

OSTEOCHONDROSIS
This increasingly diagnosed condition, in which areas of joint cartilage "die", usually first affects puppies between four and eight months old. It may occur in any joint, but Goldens suffer most frequently in the elbows, causing pain-induced lameness that leads to arthritis in later life. Causal factors include genetic make-up, hormone imbalance, diet, and exercise. Diagnosed by X-ray, treatment may involve surgical removal of floating cartilage from the joint.

DEAFNESS
Deafness is not uncommon in older Goldens. Arthritic changes may occur in the middle ear and nerve transmission to the brain gradually diminishes. Fortunately, Goldens are fairly adept at learning sign language.

BRAIN

MIDDLE EAR

SPINAL COLUMN

INTESTINES

RECTUM

SHOULDER JOINT

STOMACH

ELBOW JOINT

IRRITABLE BOWEL SYNDROME
Goldens are prone to a higher than average incidence of colitis, an inflammation of the large intestine frequently caused by food. Affected dogs will often get diarrhoea – with mucus and occasionally blood – and may suffer vomiting. Prescribed medication with strict dietary control should alleviate the problem.

FORESEEING DANGERS

NEVER ASSUME THAT your dog has the common sense to avoid dangers; even the best-trained Golden Retriever – if overexcited – may dart onto the road or jump into dangerous waters. Monitor your dog while it is outdoors, and do not leave it alone in situations where it may imperil itself or others.

ENSURING SAFETY WITH YOUR LIVELY GOLDEN

INSTILLING ROAD SENSE
Walk your Golden on a lead beside a busy road, or in places where different dangers exist. Keep tight control, because if a driver swerves to avoid your dog, any damage caused may be your legal responsibility. It is advisable to insure yourself against liability for your Golden Retriever's actions.

POTENTIAL HAZARDS IN WATER
The Golden Retriever is a natural swimmer, but always make sure that your Golden can get in and out of the water with ease and safety. Be wary of water-borne diseases such as leptospirosis, spread by infected rat urine, and blue-green algae bloom, which may cause itchy skin, diarrhoea, and even death. Avoid icy waters – your Golden's thick coat may not be enough to prevent hypothermia.

CONTROLLING AN INQUISITIVE NATURE
Watch your Golden carefully whenever it exercises off its lead. Curious dogs are more prone to injury, and exploratory wanders or investigative digging can result in bites from other animals, stings, and irritations caused by plants or insects. Do not allow your dog to eat animal droppings, or soft bones – if swallowed they may block the intestines, sometimes necessitating surgery. Always carry a first-aid kit to treat any minor injuries.

COMMON POISONS AND CONTAMINANTS

IF INGESTED		ACTION
Slug and snail bait Strychnine rat poison Illegal drugs Aspirin and other painkillers Sedatives and antidepressants	Warfarin rat poison Lead (batteries, etc.) Antifreeze	Examine any packaging to determine its contents. If the poison was swallowed within the last two hours, induce vomiting by giving crystals of washing soda, a "ball" of wet salt, or 3 per cent hydrogen peroxide by mouth. Consult your vet immediately.
Caustic soda Dishwasher granules Paint remover or thinner Kerosene or petrol Drain, toilet, or oven cleaner	Chlorine bleach Laundry detergents Wood preservatives Polishes	Do not induce vomiting. Give raw egg white, bicarbonate of soda, charcoal powder, or olive oil by mouth. Apply a paste of bicarbonate of soda to any burns in the mouth. Seek urgent medical advice from your veterinarian.

IF IN CONTACT WITH THE COAT	ACTION
Paint Tar Petroleum products Motor oil	Do not apply paint remover or concentrated biological detergents. Wearing protective gloves, rub plenty of liquid paraffin or vegetable oil into the coat. Bathe with warm, soapy water or baby shampoo. Rub in flour to help absorb the poison.
Anything other than paint, tar, petroleum products, and motor oil	Wearing protective gloves, flush the affected area for at least five minutes, using plenty of clean, tepid water. Then bathe the contaminated coat thoroughly with warm, soapy water or mild, non-irritating baby shampoo.

EMERGENCY TREATMENT

With any case of poisoning, look for signs of shock, and give essential first aid as required. Contact your vet or local poison-control centre for specific advice, and begin home treatment as quickly as possible, preferably under professional guidance by telephone.

STORE ALL TOXINS SECURELY

Chewing is a favourite pastime for all puppies and adult dogs, so keep all household, garden, and swimming-pool chemicals stored safely out of sight and reach. Never give your Golden Retriever an empty container as a toy, because it will not be able to differentiate between this and a harmful one – with potentially lethal results.

PROTECTION FROM ELECTRICAL HAZARDS

Puppies naturally gnaw anything, and often find the texture of electric flex particularly appealing. Train your dog from an early age not to tamper with electrical apparatus, and reduce the risk of burns or electrocution by placing electrical cords out of reach or spraying them with bitter-tasting aerosol. Switch off sockets when not in use and, if possible, add protective covers. If your Golden does chew through a live cable, do not risk your own life. Turn off the main electricity supply before administering first aid.

EMERGENCY FIRST AID

EVERYDAY MINOR INJURIES can be successfully treated at home with a standard first-aid kit. Emergencies of a more serious nature are thankfully much less common but, equipped with knowledge of the basic principles and techniques of artificial respiration and cardiac massage, you could save your dog's life.

FIRST-AID PRINCIPLES AND BASIC EQUIPMENT

In the event of a crisis, your objectives are to preserve life, prevent further injury, control damage, minimize pain and distress, promote healing, and get your dog safely to a veterinarian for professional care. The fundamentals of human first aid also apply to dogs. Have a fully-stocked first-aid kit handy and use it to treat minor wounds, once you are certain there are no more serious, life-threatening problems to deal with.

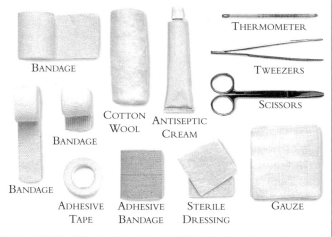

BANDAGE

BANDAGE

BANDAGE

COTTON WOOL

ANTISEPTIC CREAM

ADHESIVE TAPE

ADHESIVE BANDAGE

STERILE DRESSING

GAUZE

THERMOMETER

TWEEZERS

SCISSORS

HOW TO ASSESS AN UNCONSCIOUS DOG

Certain incidents could lead to your dog losing consciousness, such as choking, electrocution, blood loss, near-drowning, poisoning, concussion, shock, fainting, smoke inhalation, diabetes, and heart failure. If your dog appears to be unconscious, call out its name and look for signs of a response. Pinch hard between the toes, while checking the eyes for blinking. Pull on a limb – does your dog pull back? Put your hand firmly on its chest and feel for a heartbeat. Lift the top lip and look at the colour of the gum. If it is pink, and when you squeeze the pinkness out it comes back immediately, your dog's heart is beating. If the gums are very pale or blue, cardiac massage may be required to restore circulation, while someone seeks veterinary assistance.

Pale or blue gums may indicate life-threatening shock

Shock can either weaken or elevate the heart rate

ARTIFICIAL RESPIRATION AND CARDIAC MASSAGE

Do not attempt to give artificial respiration or heart massage unless your dog is unconscious and will die without your help. If your dog has been pulled from water, suspend it by its hind legs for at least 30 seconds to drain the air passages. If it has been electrocuted, do not touch it until the electricity is turned off. If it has choked, press forcefully over the ribs to dislodge the object. Never put yourself at risk; if possible, share first-aid procedures with someone else or have them telephone the nearest veterinarian and arrange transport.

Tongue is pulled forwards and debris removed

1 Place your dog on its side, ideally with its head slightly lower than the rest of its body – elevation of the hindquarters sends more blood to the brain. Clear the airway by straightening the neck, pulling the tongue fully forwards, and sweeping the mouth with two fingers to remove any excess saliva or obstructions. Also ensure that the nose is not clogged with mucus or debris. If you cannot hear the heart, start cardiac massage at once.

Extend neck to open airways to the lungs

2 Hold the muzzle shut with both hands, and place your mouth around the nose. Blow in until you see the chest expand, then let the lungs naturally deflate. Repeat this 10–20 times per minute, checking the pulse every 10 seconds to make sure the heart is beating.

Pumping forces blood towards brain

ALWAYS LOOK FOR SHOCK

Shock is a potentially life-endangering condition which occurs when the body's circulation fails. It can be caused by vomiting, diarrhoea, poisons, animal bites, a twisted stomach, bleeding, and many other illnesses or accidents, and onset may not be apparent for several hours. The signs include pale or blue gums, rapid breathing, a faint or quickened pulse, cold extremities, and general weakness. Treating shock takes precedence over other injuries, including fractures. Your priorities are to control any bleeding, maintain body heat, and support vital functions. Unless shock is the result of heatstroke, wrap your dog loosely in a warm blanket, elevate its hindquarters, stabilize breathing and the heart if necessary using mouth-to-nose resuscitation and cardiac massage, and seek urgent medical advice.

3 If the heart has stopped, begin cardiac massage immediately. Place the heel of one hand on the left side of the chest just behind the elbow, then the heel of your other hand on top. Press vigorously down and forwards, pumping 80–100 times per minute. Alternate 20–25 cardiac massages with 10 seconds of mouth-to-nose respiration until the heart beats, restoring colour to the gums. Continue resuscitation until breathing starts. A very fat Golden should be laid on its back and pressed on the chest for cardiac massage.

MINOR INJURY AND ILLNESS

THE MOST COMMON INJURIES that Goldens suffer are cuts to their paws from sharp objects, and wounds to their ears from dog bites. Both injuries can bleed profusely and may need bandaging before veterinary treatment. Every owner should know how to administer basic treatment to their dog.

APPLYING AN EMERGENCY BANDAGE TO THE EAR

Assistant holds pad in place

1 While an assistant soothes and steadies your dog, apply clean, preferably non-stick, absorbent material to the wound. Take care you are not bitten through fright. Cut a section from a pair of tights and slip it over your hands.

2 Give verbal reassurance while slipping the "tube bandage" over your dog's nose and onto its ear. This will hold the pad firmly onto the bleeding wound. Ensure that the windpipe receives no undue pressure.

BANDAGING A WOUNDED PAW

Wrapping too tightly can restrict circulation to leg

Kneeling behind, assistant keeps injured dog still

To control bleeding, apply a blotting-type pad to the cut, wrap the pad with stretchy gauze, and secure the dressing in place with clinging stretch or adhesive bandage. Consult your vet about antibiotics or possible surgery. Change bandages daily to reduce the risk of infection.

3 You can secure the tights at each end with adhesive tape to prevent your dog from dislodging the bandage. This breathable material allows air in to clot the blood, making it an ideal temporary cover.

IMPROVISING A MUZZLE

Unless breathing is impaired, apply muzzle for safety

1 Even the most loving animal is capable of reflex biting if in pain. To avoid this during first-aid treatment, make a loop with soft material such as tights or a tie, and with the aid of a helper, slip it over the muzzle.

2 With the loop in place, tighten it gently. Then bring both lengths of material down and cross them under the jaws. If your dog is confused or upset, speak to it in a relaxed, comforting tone as you proceed.

3 To complete the process, wrap the material around the back of the ears and tie the ends securely in a knot. With the emergency muzzle securely fastened, you can then safely examine and treat the injured area.

ADMINISTERING MEDICINES

Pill can be hidden in food

GIVING A PILL

With your dog seated, open its mouth and insert the pill as far back as possible. Then hold the jaw shut and tilt it upwards, stroking the neck to induce swallowing.

Cough syrup is taken easily from syringe

GIVING LIQUIDS

If you cannot mix the medicine in food, use a syringe to squirt it into the mouth, not down the throat where it may enter the windpipe. Hold the muzzle shut until it swallows.

USING AN ELIZABETHAN COLLAR

Your vet may provide a lampshade-shaped collar for your convalescent dog, to prevent any scratching or chewing at wounds. This collar should be left on whenever your dog is alone, but may be removed at mealtimes or during exercise on a lead, when you can deter self-inflicted damage. Although it is in the dog's best interests, the device is cumbersome and likely to be worn without enthusiasm.

EARLY BREED ORIGINS

DOGS HAVE ASSISTED in hunting for thousands of years. The Golden Retriever – a modern sporting dog – probably originated from the large spaniels that spread from Spain throughout Europe up to 1,000 years ago, and with human intervention evolved into today's variety of pointers, setters, and retrievers.

FIRST RETRIEVERS

EARLY SPORTING DOGS

RETRIEVING ANCESTORS

The first European sporting dogs were innate hunters, using their nose to scent-trail game, and their speed to capture it. By the Middle Ages, both setters and pointers had evolved; dogs that tracked game, but then "froze" rather than chasing and attacking. Originally, game birds were caught by nets. When hunting with guns became a pastime of the wealthy, a need emerged for a soft-mouthed breed capable of retrieving shot birds from land and water.

ARISTOCRATIC INFLUENCES

Hunting merely for sport was restricted to the very wealthy. They bred and raised thousands of birds, driven by "beaters" to the gun on shooting days. These competitive sportsmen bred their own lines of setters and retrievers – many are now extinct, but the gentle, obedient Golden Retriever flourished.

TRADITIONAL SHOOTING SCENE

FOUNDER BREEDS

PORTUGUESE WATER DOG

The Golden Retriever's early origins can be traced back to various breeds, perhaps starting with Portuguese and Spanish Water Dogs. These specialized dogs, with waterproof coats and innate retrieving instinct, voyaged with fishermen to the cod fishery off Newfoundland in Canada. At the same time, fishermen from southwest England settled in Newfoundland, also with their dogs. The root stock of all modern retrievers developed from this disparate mix of dogs. The Golden Retriever is probably a cross between a Flat-coated Retriever and the now-extinct Tweed Water Spaniel, with some Irish Setter blood introduced at a later stage.

TWEED WATER SPANIEL
Along the Scottish coasts, water spaniels were used for retrieving fowl. Belle – a Tweed Water Spaniel – was integral in developing today's Golden Retriever

THE RUSSIAN CIRCUS STORY

For many years, it was widely believed that the Golden Retriever originated from a troupe of Russian circus dogs, purchased by the first Lord Tweedmouth. Some early breeders even travelled to the Russian Caucasus Mountains in search of new bloodlines. However, archive kennel records show that Lord Tweedmouth acquired the only yellow retriever in a litter of black wavy-coats from a Brighton cobbler around 1860, and he named this dog Nous. It is documented that a liver-coloured Tweed Water Spaniel named Belle was bred to Nous, producing four yellow puppies. These dogs were then bred to create the Golden Retriever breed. While there are Russian sheepdogs, and breeds such as the Hovawart which look like large versions of the Golden Retriever, their personalities are much more territorial, guarded, and suspicious.

WAVY-COATED RETRIEVER
This dog, Nous, sired the first Golden Retriever breeding line

GREATER ST. JOHN'S DOGS (FIRST NEWFOUNDLAND)
This ancestor of the Flat-coated, Labrador, and Golden Retrievers provided invaluable assistance to early fishermen

IRISH SETTER
An Irish Setter was mated to Cowslip (one of four puppies produced by Belle and Nous). The offspring played an important role in the early development of the Golden Retriever

RECENT HISTORY

THE GOLDEN RETRIEVER is such a modern breed that the names of the original dogs and pioneering breeders can be easily found. Today's Golden still resembles those early dogs in both looks and personality, but these attributes have been enhanced even further, to ensure its working potential and enduring appeal.

DEVELOPMENT OF THE MODERN GOLDEN

THE FIRST GOLDEN RETRIEVER LITTER

At his fine Scottish home, Lord Tweedmouth mated his dog Nous to Belle (a Tweed Water Spaniel), producing, in 1868, four yellow puppies – Ada, Cowslip, Crocus, and Primrose – all strongly resembling modern-day Goldens. Later, he mated Cowslip to a different Tweed Water Spaniel to advance the Golden Retriever line.

ENGLISH FIELD TRIALS

In 1904, a "liver flat-coat" descendant of Ada won a retriever field trial. Goldens were first exhibited at the Crystal Palace Dog Show in 1908, as "Flat-coats, Golden". The title "Golden Retriever" was introduced in 1920.

PROMINENT BREEDERS

The Victorian aristocracy was a very close-knit society and Lord Tweedmouth quickly dispersed his yellow retrievers among his friends' country estates. Breeding of this delightful dog remained in their hands until well into the 20th century.

EARLY MIGRATION

In 1894, Lord Tweedmouth's son and Lady, his Golden, migrated to Texas via Canada. The breed had spread internationally by the 1930s, and today it enjoys worldwide popularity.

NEAREST RELATIVES

Several modern breeds share a common ancestry with the Golden Retriever. All of these dogs have been selectively bred for their even temper, desire to please, and "soft mouth" retrieving. Goldens tend to live the longest of all the retrievers.

CURLY-COATED RETRIEVER
Relatively rare today, this breed was brought to the United Kingdom by cod fishermen. It has a water dog's coat, composed of crisp, tight, small, waterproof curls

FLAT-COATED RETRIEVER
This is thought to be the Golden's immediate ancestor, although it is leaner, with a livelier, almost setter-like, temperament

LABRADOR RETRIEVER
Another descendant of Lesser St. John's Dogs, it shares a similar working role and personality with its distant relative, the Golden Retriever

CHESAPEAKE BAY RETRIEVER
This dog is the result of Lesser St. John's Dogs bred with local American hounds

NEWFOUNDLAND
Derived from the Greater Newfoundland or St. John's Dog, it is a large, happy breed, and is still used for assistance work in water

REPRODUCTION

ANATOMICALLY, BOTH MALE and female Golden Retrievers are well constructed and seldom have problems producing a litter. However, the decision to mate your dog must be made responsibly as Golden litters are often large. Seek medical advice before mating and enlist help during the delivery.

THE MATING INSTINCT

A healthy male can be used for mating as young as 10 months old. It is best to wait until a female is two years of age – usually in her third oestrous cycle – when she is emotionally prepared for a litter. Ovulation tends to occur 10–12 days after the first sign of bleeding and vulvar swelling. Take the female to the male's home, where he is more likely to perform as expected!

PREGNANCY DIAGNOSIS

Ovulation – the prime time for conception – is accurately assessed by an increased level of the hormone progesterone in the blood. Pregnancy, however, cannot be confirmed by either blood or urine tests. An ultrasound scan at three weeks or a physical examination slightly later are the best means of diagnosis.

Ultrasound scan shows several puppies in womb

DEALING WITH MISMATING

Mismatings can be avoided by keeping a watchful eye on your bitch when in season, by using tablets or injections to prevent ovulation, or by spaying. If an unwanted mating does occur, contact your vet. A pregnancy can be terminated, usually within three days of mating, with a hormone injection. This will induce an immediate repeat season, demanding renewed vigilance for 8–15 days after the beginning of vaginal discharge.

SPECIAL NEEDS OF AN EXPECTANT BITCH

During the first month of pregnancy, a bitch should continue to exercise freely. Thereafter, the increasing weight of the litter will naturally make her slower and less agile. At this stage, swimming is good exercise, but avoid very cold water. After the sixth week, gradually increase food quantities until the birth, so that her diet contains 30 per cent more than her usual daily intake. This should include an adequate amount of calcium.

MALE AND FEMALE REPRODUCTIVE SYSTEMS

A bitch comes into season twice yearly, is fertile for three days during each cycle, and will be receptive to mating only during these periods. Males, however, willingly mate all year round. For the female, ovulation continues throughout life and there is no menopause, although breeding in later years is risky. Pregnancy lasts for about 63 days.

RESPONSIBLE BREEDING

Never produce a litter of puppies if they are unwanted or likely to be unwell. Before breeding from your Golden, seek professional advice from your vet or from a breeder. Ensure that both prospective parents' physical and emotional attributes will enhance the breed, and that they have been screened for inherited diseases such as progressive retinal atrophy and hip dysplasia. Your vet may also advise testing for brucellosis, a canine venereal disease. Remember that you are responsible for finding safe homes for the offspring.

PREVENTING PREGNANCY

Neutering is the most effective and safest means of preventing pregnancy. The female, because she carries the young, is the usual candidate. Both the ovaries and the uterus are removed, followed by a week's rest. The procedure for males involves simple surgery on the scrotum for removal of the testicles.

MALE

KIDNEY

BLADDER

TESTICLE

PENIS

FEMALE

UTERUS

VAGINA

VULVA

BLADDER

UTERINE HORN

OVARY

KIDNEY

PRE- AND POST-WHELPING

INTRODUCE THE EXPECTANT mother to her whelping box in readiness for the new litter. Watch closely for the signs of labour and arrange for your vet to be on call in case of problems. Goldens rarely experience difficulties, but professional help is useful during the delivery, and for the after-care of weak puppies.

INTRODUCING A WHELPING BOX

A few weeks before she is due to deliver, familiarize the mother-to-be with her whelping box. The box should have a length and width of at least 1.2 m (4 ft), and be made of marine ply, which will not be damaged by birth fluids. Three sides should be 45–50 cm (18–20 in) high to prevent the puppies from escaping, while the fourth should have a lockable opening to allow the mother easy access. Collect bundles of newspaper to line the box and to serve as bedding for the puppies.

Expectant mother happily accepts purpose-made whelping box

DELIVERY CARE

If you have never been present at a birth, ask an experienced dog breeder to attend, and inform your vet when labour begins. Keep the room temperature at around 25° C (77° F). If after two hours your bitch does not produce a puppy, contact your vet once again for advice. The puppy's position may need manipulating to facilitate delivery. Although rare, some Goldens do require a Caesarean section. Place a warm, towel-covered hot-water bottle in a cardboard box, and use this as a safe receptacle for each newly-delivered puppy. You may also use this box to transport the puppies if mother and litter need to visit the vet.

SIGNS OF IMPENDING BIRTH

Shortly before going into labour your bitch will probably refuse food. She will seek out her whelping box and start to tear up the bedding, preparing a nest for her puppies. Her body temperature will drop, and she may pant. Birth is imminent when her contractions begin and a membrane balloon appears in her vulva. Keep other animals and strangers away.

THE NEW LITTER

After delivery, towel-dry each puppy and clear its nose of mucus; it should then squeal and wriggle. Place each newborn by a teat to suckle. During whelping, offer the mother drinks of warm milk. Let her rest after the placentas have been delivered, but do not be alarmed if she bears one last puppy! Start to increase food quantities – at peak lactation up to four times her normal daily intake.

Puppies clamber over each other to reach mother's teats

ASSISTING A WEAK OR ABANDONED PUPPY

HELPING TO SUCKLE

On average, one out of seven puppies is born relatively small and weak. Runts are often the least healthy of the litter, and if left to nature frequently die within a few days. To aid survival, place a frail puppy near the teats offering the best supply of milk.

BOTTLE-FEEDING

In large, healthy litters where there simply is not enough milk to feed all the puppies, or when the mother is incapacitated or abandons her offspring, use canine milk formula as a supplement. Bottle-feed initially every two to three hours, seeking your vet's guidance on the correct quantities.

GROWING TOGETHER

The most important learning period for all dogs is during the first three months of life. After three weeks, the puppies' senses start to develop rapidly, and they begin to explore. Handle and groom all puppies often, so they learn to accept being touched, but do not upset the protective mother. Gentle exposure to new sights and sounds at this stage will help the puppies to grow into well-adjusted adults.

PARTICIPATING IN A SHOW

TAKING PART IN a dog show can be great fun for both you and your dog, but it requires careful preparation and training. From informal competitions to exclusive Golden championships, your dog will be evaluated against a breed standard of ideal physical and personality characteristics, which typify the "perfect" specimen.

MEETING SHOW STANDARDS

Visit shows without your dog to see exactly what happens. While working trials require dogs well trained in obedience, or with more specialized skills, kennel club events demand only personality and beauty. For these, your dog must (at least in your eyes) meet the published breed standard. It should be confident, enjoy being handled by strangers, and ideally be a bit of a show-off!

This naturally handsome dog receives a last-minute spruce

STANDING FOR INSPECTION

Wait for your cue, then enter the ring and set your Golden in its "show stance". The judge will examine the body – feeling the joints, muscles, and looking in the mouth – to see how your dog compares to the breed standard. At the same time, your dog's temperament is being noted. Aggressive or fearful dogs never reach the final line-up.

PREPARING FOR THE SHOW

In addition to the practical pre-show arrangements, ensure your Golden is in peak physical condition, with clean teeth and wax-free ears. Bathe your dog a few days before a show to allow renewal of the coat's sheen by natural oils – use coat conditioner only when advised by experienced exhibitors. Clip the nails and trim excess feathering from the feet, legs, and tail. No cosmetic or surgical aids to improve your dog's looks are permitted.

ENJOYING THE DAY

Participating in dog shows should be enjoyable for you, your family, and your Golden. At the highest levels of showing, breeders take shows very seriously and employ professional handlers. At all other levels, these events should be viewed as an enjoyable hobby, offering friendly competition and the chance to socialize with like-minded people. Winning, of course, would be an added bonus.

ASSESSMENT OF THE GAIT

After the physical examination, the judge will ask for each dog to be walked around the ring, to appraise its movement. Golden Retrievers usually "gait" with confidence and fluid grace, but any signs of hesitancy will be penalized. The judge will also assess how well you work with your dog; the better the symmetry between you both, the higher the score will be. This is why professional handlers are used in major shows. Goldens who are very self-assured will relish the chance to parade in the limelight.

BEST OF BREED CHAMPION

After individual assessments, the judge will choose a shortlist of six or seven dogs. These are examined again, then placed in order of merit, with the judge awarding rosettes for first, second, and third place, as well as for "reserve" and "highly commended" contenders. Ideal looks and show style are not the sole criteria of an outstanding Golden – any dog in glowing health and with a fine temperament is a fine example of the breed.

COSTS OF SHOWING

Showing your own Golden Retriever is relatively cheap; your only expenses are entry fees, transport, and accommodation. However, costs can increase dramatically if you employ a professional handler, as it is a rare dog that is so successful that handling costs are earned back in stud fees or puppy prices. Unless you are interested in serious exhibiting, it is far better to approach showing your Golden as a pleasurable but minor activity for you and your dog.

SPECIALIZED TRAINING

ONE OF THE WORLD's favourite household companions, the Golden Retriever is also an efficient worker. Whether taking part in a hunt, field trial, or advanced obedience or agility competition, the Golden's strong retrieval instinct, scenting ability, and "soft mouth" make it a multipurpose breed.

FIELD AND HUNTING ROLES

WORKING TO THE GUN

Even if your Golden is adept at retrieving, it will need supervision from an experienced trainer for introduction to gunfire, tracking, and tenderly collecting freshly-killed game. Join a local gundog club to master relevant verbal, whistle, and directional commands, and perhaps a tracking club for advice on training your dog to follow a scent trail. On its first successful retrieve in the field, your Golden will be as thrilled and excited as you are.

Game is returned to owner's hand

SELECTING THE RIGHT PUPPY FOR TRAINING

All Goldens share an inborn desire to retrieve, and have been bred to respond well to human direction. They are also "soft mouthed" – able to hold items gently. With tuition, most Goldens can be trained in advanced obedience, agility, or gunwork. However, various kennels specialize in producing dogs for different roles, especially field trials and the show ring. Field trials require nimbleness, swift response to command, and highly developed scenting skills. If you plan to enter this competitive sport, seek advice from a successful field-trial trainer on selecting the most suitable puppy.

RETRIEVE TRAINING

After training your Golden to walk to heel, begin retrieve training in a hallway with a canvas-covered dummy. The desire to retrieve is strong, but the instinct to do so must be cultured indoors, graduating outside to unfamiliar terrain and the distractions of a field trial or hunt situation.

ADVANCED OBEDIENCE TRIALS

SUSTAINED LIE-DOWN ON COMMAND

Competitive obedience trials provide excellent mental stimulation. Start classes at six months, after your dog has mastered basic commands and walking on a lead. Advanced training includes close and fast-pace heelwork, retrieves, recalls, distant control, sustained sit-downs (sometimes for as long as 10 minutes with the handler out of sight), send away-down-return sequences, and scent discrimination.

RETRIEVING A DUMBBELL
Goldens thrive on retrieval tests, as they have a natural advantage over many breeds. Beginning with a dumbbell, dogs progress to fetching items provided by the trials judges.

TRAINING IN AGILITY

NEGOTIATING OBSTACLES
Agility courses are run "against the clock". Although Goldens are not as fast as some other breeds, they can be very accurate if enthusiasm is curbed.

TIPPING A SEE-SAW

Agility exercises require dexterity, confidence, and instant response to command, and can be a productive channel for restless energy. Standard trial apparatus includes an "A" frame, hurdles, a tyre, poles to weave through, a tunnel, and a see-saw. Training demands ample patience. To be successful, your dog must respond well off the lead and tackle any obstacle on your command. Start when your dog is a year old by enrolling at a local club. Make sure that both you and your Golden are fit enough to participate.

ASSISTANCE ROLES

ALTHOUGH A RELATIVELY new breed, the Golden Retriever's working potential was recognized early in its development. Over the years, carefully devised breeding programmes have advanced the Golden's innate attributes, so that it is now a popular choice as a guide dog for the blind and other assistance roles.

BRED AND TRAINED AS A HELPING COMPANION

EARLY PUPPY TRAINING
Golden Retrievers, Labradors, and their cross-breeds are the most popular guide dogs for the blind. The largest guide-dog training centres breed their own stock, although some small kennels produce very good dogs. Puppies live in volunteers' homes, where they receive basic training and exposure to various learning situations.

TRAINING AS A GUIDE DOG
The Golden's medium size, eagerness to please, receptiveness to training and, above all, its steady temperament, make it ideal for assistance work. Selective breeding ensures that individuals are calm and sensible in unusual situations, which has led to a low drop-out rate – less than 30 per cent – during the months of intensive training at guide-dog centres. Goldens tend to be very affectionate, which is an added bonus for the eventual recipient.

Watchful and obedient, this Golden guide dog awaits instruction

EYES FOR THE BLIND
To ensure lasting success, it is important that the guide dog and owner have compatible personalities. Both parties undergo a period of residential training to learn to understand each other, which is followed up later by regular home visits.

MOBILITY OF THE DISABLED

The Golden's exceptional skills can be channelled to meet the specific needs of its disabled owner – to pull a wheelchair, open certain types of door, stand and push lift buttons, or even to open clothes dryers and take out the washing! These actions may attract the interest of strangers, making the owner more readily approachable for general conversation.

CROSS-BRED FOR IMPROVED HEALTH

As its personality is similar to that of the Golden, the Labrador Retriever is also used in a vast range of service capacities, as a guide dog for the blind and helping the disabled and infirm in assistance roles. To reduce the risk of breed-related genetic disorders – ranging from arthritis to blindness – the two breeds are often crossed, producing puppies that are both temperamentally sound and less prone to inherited ailments.

INVALUABLE HOME HELP

Goldens naturally carry objects and can easily be trained to fetch household items to help the infirm and disabled. Particularly gregarious individuals can act as ears for deaf people, alerting their owners to important sounds, such as a doorbell ringing or baby crying. Young guide dogs that prove too active for the role are often retrained as "hearing dogs".

Specially-designed case allows Golden to hold telephone in its mouth

Patient enjoys lavish attention from genuinely friendly Golden

HOSPITAL COMPANION

In many countries, the Golden Retriever is used as a "therapy dog", taken on routine visits to hospitals and institutions where there are no facilities to keep residential dogs. Goldens are ideal for this role because they enjoy giving and receiving attention, and are large enough to be stroked by people restricted to a chair. Medical personnel are constantly surprised by the visible improvements seen in their patients, and welcome these visits as much as the residents and the dogs themselves.

BREED STANDARD

A BREED STANDARD is used by the governing kennel club of each country to describe the ideal Golden Retriever. Show dogs are judged against this formal index of the unique physical qualities, demeanour, and personality traits that characterize a "perfect" specimen of the breed.

GOLDEN RETRIEVER
GUNDOG GROUP
(Last revised March 1994)

Reproduced by kind permission of
The Kennel Club
London, England

GENERAL APPEARANCE
Symmetrical, balanced, active, powerful, level mover; sound with kindly expression.

CHARACTERISTICS
Biddable, intelligent and possessing natural working ability.

TEMPERAMENT
Kindly, friendly and confident.

HEAD AND SKULL
Balanced and well chiselled, skull broad without coarseness; well set on neck, muzzle powerful, wide and deep. Length of foreface approximately equals length from well defined stop to occiput. Nose preferably black.

EYES
Dark brown, set well apart, dark rims.

EARS
Moderate size, set on approximate level with eyes.

MOUTH
Jaws strong, with a perfect, regular and complete scissor bite, i.e. upper teeth closely overlapping lower teeth and set square to the jaws.

NECK
Good length, clean and muscular.

FOREQUARTERS
Forelegs straight with good bone, shoulders well laid back, long in blade with upper arm of equal length placing legs well under body. Elbows close fitting.

BODY
Balanced, short-coupled, deep through heart. Ribs deep, well sprung. Level topline.

HINDQUARTERS
Loin and legs strong and muscular, good second thighs, well bent stifles. Hocks well let down, straight when viewed from rear, neither turning in nor out. Cow-hocks highly undesirable.

FEET
Round and cat-like.

TAIL
Set on and carried level with back, reaching to hocks, without curl at tip.

GAIT/MOVEMENT
Powerful with good drive. Straight and true in front and rear. Stride long and free with no sign of hackney action in front.

COAT
Flat or wavy with good feathering, dense water-resisting undercoat.

COLOUR
Any shade of gold or cream, neither red nor mahogany. A few white hairs on chest only, permissible.

SIZE
Height at withers:
dogs: 56–61 cms (22–24 ins);
bitches: 51–56 cms (20–22 ins).

FAULTS
Any departure from the foregoing points should be considered a fault and the seriousness with which the fault should be regarded should be in exact proportion to its degree.

NOTE
Male animals should have two apparently normal testicles fully descended into the scrotum.

GLOSSARY

COW-HOCKED When the hocks turn inwards towards each other.

ELBOW The joint between the upper arm and the forearm.

FEATHERING Longer fringe of hair on ears, legs, tail, or body.

FOREARM The bone of the forelegs between elbow and wrist.

FORELEG The front leg from elbow to foot.

FOREQUARTERS Front part of dog excluding head and neck.

GAIT The pattern of footsteps at various rates of speed, each pattern distinguished by a particular rhythm and footfall.

GUNDOG A dog trained to work to find live game and/or retrieve game that has been shot or wounded.

HACKNEY ACTION The high lifting action of the front feet.

HIND LEG Leg from pelvis to foot.

HINDQUARTERS Rear part of dog from loin.

HOCK The tarsus or collection of bones of the hind leg forming the joint between the second thigh and the metatarsus.

LOIN Region of the body on either side of vertebral column between the last ribs and the hindquarters.

METATARSALS Bones between the hock joint and foot.

MUZZLE The head in front of the eyes, nasal bone, nostrils, and jaws; foreface.

OCCIPUT Upper, back point of skull.

SHORT-COUPLED With very short coupling. [The part of the body between the ribs and pelvis; the loin.]

SKULL Bony regions of head. Usually meant as section of head from stop to occiput.

SOFT MOUTH Gentle grip on a retrieve.

STIFLE The joint of the hind leg between the thigh and the second thigh; the dog's knee.

STOP The step up from muzzle to skull; indentation between the eyes where the nasal bone and skull meet.

TOPLINE The dog's outline from just behind the withers to the tail set.

UNDERCOAT Dense, soft, short coat concealed by longer top-coat.

WELL SPRUNG RIBS Ribs springing out from spinal column giving correct shape.

WITHERS The highest point of the body, immediately behind the neck.

INDEX

ACKNOWLEDGMENTS

AUTHOR'S ACKNOWLEDGMENTS
Many thanks to Phil Hunt, Sarah Lillicrapp, Wendy Bartlet, Helen Thompson and their efficient DK production team, and to Patricia Holden White for choreographing several photographic sessions. Further thanks to Dr. Gary Clayton Jones for X-rays of joint disease, Dr. Sheila Crispin at the University of Bristol's Department of Clinical Veterinary Science for information and photographs of Golden Retriever inherited eye problems, Dr. Peter Kertesz for data on teeth, and Dr. Ivan Burger at the Waltham Centre for Pet Nutrition for detailed advice on the Golden Retriever's energy requirements. Finally, my thanks to the veterinarians worldwide who have helped with information on Golden Retriever behaviour.

PUBLISHER'S ACKNOWLEDGMENTS
Dorling Kindersley would like to thank photographer Tracy Morgan for her invaluable contribution to the book. Also special thanks to Tracy's photographic assistants: K. Cuthbert, Sally Bergh-Roose, and Stella Smyth-Carpenter. We are also very grateful to Patricia Holden White for her generous advice and help on photographic sessions, and to Karin Woodruff for the index. A very special thank you to all the staff of the Guide Dogs for the Blind Association (Breeding Centre), Tollgate House, Warwickshire, especially to Neil Ewart and Helen Freeman, whose expert guidance, tireless assistance, and endless supply of puppies were crucial in completing several sections of the book. Finally, we would like to thank the following people for lending their dogs and/or for modelling:

Kane Andrews; Wendy Bartlet; Sally Bergh-Roose; Mrs. V. Clarke; Sue Cox; Kuryan M. Cuthbert; Mr. and Mrs. Denham and "Oscar" (Glenrod Nimrod); Bruce Fogle; Helen Freeman; Gloria Gargan and Siagar Recherche; Mr. and Mrs. Gordon and "Abbi"; Guide Dogs for the Blind Association, "Jamie", "Rowena", and various puppies; Phil Hunt; Shirley Liles, "Tamar" (Fadius Mystic Lad) and "Amy" (Tugwood Jenetta); Sarah Lillicrapp; Linda, Robert, and Gemma Marcham, "Amber" (Culray Amberfire of Chapledown), "Jake" (Chapledown Bystander), "Sam" (Bridgefarm Irwin of Chapledown), "Cassie" (Culray Castelle), and "Jessica" (Lindymar Jessica); Daniel McCarthy; Mr. and Mrs. R. Rains, "Thomas" (Champion Millgreen Magnum), "Sunny" (Catcombe Carbon Copy), "Remy" (Narside You've Got It), and "Wilson" (Stanrope Soft Shoe Shuffle); Dee Roth-Brown and her agility Golden; Hesta Small; Stella and Stephanie Smyth-Carpenter; Sandra Stephens, "Poppy" (Hampdenlea Honey Flower), "Annie" (Hampdenlea Clover Leaf), "Katie" (Starlance Dian), and "Daisy" (Hampdenlea Moon Daisy); Mr. and Mrs. Studwick; Helen Thompson; Lyn Ward; Pat Woodbridge and "Toby" (Pepsanner Victor Hugo).

PHOTOGRAPHIC CREDITS
Every effort has been made to trace the copyright holders, and we apologize in advance for any unintentional omissions. We would be pleased to insert the appropriate acknowledgments in any subsequent edition of this publication.

Key: l=left, r=right, t=top, c=centre, a=above, b=below

All photography by Tracy Morgan except:
Animal Photography: (Sally Anne Thompson) 69tl; (R. Willbie) 15br; **Christopher Bradbury:** 66cr, 69cl, 69cr; **Bridgeman Art Library, London:** (Christie's, London) 6cr; **Dr. Sheila Crispin:** 54cr; **John Darling:** 2, 9tl, 72cl; **Dogs for the Disabled Association:** 7cr, 75tl, 75cr, 75bl; **Guide Dogs for the Blind Association:** 74cl, 74br; **Dr. Peter Kertesz:** 46br; **Dave King:** 15c, 16cr; **Mary Evans Picture Library:** 62cl, 62cr, 63tl, 63cr; **NHPA:** (Gerard Lacz) 6bl; **Tim Ridley:** 18b, 19tl, 38tr, 38cl, 41tr, 41cr, 41bl, 42–43, 34tl, 51tr, 70tl; **Science Photo Library:** (David Scharf) 52cl, (Sinclair Stammers) 52bl; **The Image Bank:** (Lynn M. Stone) 6tl; **David Ward:** 7tl, 8bl, 13tl, 14bl, 22bl, 26bl, 34cl, 36cl, 44br, 49cl, 51bl; **Wood Green Animal Shelters:** 19c; **Zefa:** 50cl.

ILLUSTRATIONS
Samantha Elmhurst: 52–53, 55, 65; **Angelika Elsebach:** 58–59; **Jane Pickering:** 35; **Clive Spong:** 11.